The
Golden
Age
OF
B.S.

Dobbs, Fred C.
The golden age of B.S.

ISBN 0-7715-9984-6

1. Canada - Social life and customs - 1945-
Anecdotes, facetiae, satire, etc.*
2. Canadian wit and humor. I. Title.

FC89.D62   971.06'44'0207   C76-017170-X
                F1021.D62

Printed and bound in Canada
1 2 3 4 5 RBW 80 79 78 77 76

The Golden Age of B.S.

by
Fred C. Dobbs

Gage Publishing

To Winnie who always stands behind her man

Contents

Introduction

By geez, I never thought I'd live to see the day when a town like Beamsville would see the enda her railway station. Course, the writing was on the wall when a train never stopped there in the last ten years. Still, it's awful tough getting it through your old noggin that even the station's going.

The way the railway's been acting in the last while . . . you could see it coming. Just as soon as they got careless bout putting paper in the washrooms, you knew right then and there they was gonna start discouraging people. By geez, you're going through Kicking Horse Pass with the old can bobbing and weaving . . . what a buzzsaw situation that is. Then you find there's no paper and of course, the suckers couldn't have cared less. Even the water cooler's been left empty. It was all there; you could see it happening.

You know when you stop and examine what's going on nowadays, like the Beamsville station . . . it's just getting wicked altogether. Remember them times when a fellow could be a real man without running around with a setta salmon-pink crotch huggers? People in the old days never used to torture you about Christmas coming up in only 169 more days. There was no such thing as "ring around the collar," or some poor old soul sitting bolt upright in the middle of the night and shouting, "O, that itch, that burning itch, I can't stand it." Life was simpler then. People wasn't afraid. There was no one whispering: "Don't be half safe." Horses didn't step up on hormones; oats and hay was good enough. Three-ply gentle tissue hadn't come in yet. And no one had the nerve to put up rows of pay toilets. Back in them days you could slip through life in your Stanfields, and keep just as loose as ashes and twice as dusty. You know what I'm talking about? I'm talking about those days before we were saddled with the golden age of bullshit. That's right! The golden age of bullshit. For that's just what we got now. So don't hold your breath and wait for any change, because you mark most of the promises you hear nowadays on ice. When did it all start? How did it all happen? How did they get such a hold on us?

Well, there just don't seem to be no letting up. In fact, it's just the other way around. The people's acting crazier all the time. It's as if some big slave driver up in the sky has got a whip and he's driving us.

Where did it all start? In my opinion it was right in downtown Toronto, in the spring of 1975. In that splendid shrine of Canadian cautiousness and American brass – the Four Seasons Sheraton Hotel. They're still rehearsing there, although they brought the first tub of frozen scrambled eggs in from Texas back in 1972. Well, I'm talking about what might've been the beginning, the birth, if you like, of the golden age of bullshit.

Now there was this outfit that invented everything from Truth Squads to half-million dollar grants for groups of three, providing they was professors, to study great Canadians like Disraeli. And they was having a fund-raising dinner. Kinda modest little affair, not what you'd call a big spread. Just a hundred bucks a plate. Now it wasn't one of them rubber-chicken circuit banquet affairs that the business and professional boys keep having every so often. But it was a fund-raising dinner. This outfit was really – I guess you could call it an alliance for power. That's what Grattan O'Leary called it in his time. You hadda get up pretty early in the morning to whip the likes of him. Anyways, this bunch pretty well figured they'd invented everything from the racehorse to sliced bread. They had more promises for all of us than the whole of the *Holy Bible*. Yeah, some of you would get it about now, cause I'm talking about the holiest of alliances – the religious order second to none, since Christianity come along, and them fellows threw the party for the birds who dreamed up the slogan – "The Meek Shall Inherit the Earth."

I'm talking about the Liberal Party of Canada.

1
The
Five-Minute
Liberal

You know, most people think all the good political jokes is made in the US of A. Well, that ain't true. Part of the golden age of bullshit is that right here in Canada we're getting Canadian jokes for – of *all* things – Canadians. That's quite a switch, ain't it? They're not even manufactured and printed in the US of A, they actually originated here, which is fantastic. Anyways, the one that comes to my mind right now . . .

There's this old fellow . . . geez, he was out on the highway there, out on the soft shoulder, trying to get a ride so's he could exercise his franchise at the advance poll pool. "Exercise your franchise!" That's a wonderful way of saying a fellow's gonna vote. Exercise your franchise – sounds more to me like a come-on for a massage parlor. There's something dirty about it, don't you think? Anyways, there he is, standing out on the highway, like a jackfool in broad daylight, thumb out in the air. By geez, he don't have two cents to rub together, don't have a pot to piss in nor window to throw it out of. All of a sudden, a big, new, shiny car comes along, a big Detroiter, pulls over to the soft shoulder, and the guy behind the wheel beckons to the old bird down the way. The old fellow's all smiles as he comes up, says, "By gosh, I'm all out of breath. Geez, it's awful good of you to stop. I was just trying to get a lift down to the Five Corners to exercise my franchise." The driver says, young fellow behind the wheel, a young ring-a-dinger, kinda Labatt's blue balloon man – the kind of fellow you'd see drinking Labatt's, earning about thirty grand a year . . . Did you ever notice anyone drinking Labatt's who looks like he's a working man? They're all people with Chris Craft launches and blue balloons to run around in, and ski lodges . . . Do you get the idea? The people who run the breweries of Canada don't ever wanna admit that the ordinary worker ever drinks up seven sixes or whatever number of pints a day. . . . Geez, I'm getting off the track. The young guy, the driver says,

"Geez, no kidding. Who you voting for?"

"Well," says the old fellow, "Conservatives." And he's real proud, you know, shoulders right back, kind of squares them, looks real expansive, sticks out his chest. Then the fellow behind the wheel says,

"Not with *my* help you ain't," and by gosh, he puts his foot on the gas and away he goes in a hail of dust, leaving the old fellow standing on the soft shoulder looking like a bigger fool than god ever told the other fellow about.

So he puts his thumb out and stops another car. Same dang thing. Driver asks where he's going, and the old fellow tells him. What are you going to do – that comes up one way or another. Finally, "O who you voting for?" Tells him, Conservatives.

"Not in my car," says the driver, drives away foot on the gas, leaving the old guy pretty dang confused.

Well, he's standing there, and geez, he's dusting off his Sunday-best suit, feeling real lonely, figures it's time to get back to the drawing board and come up with a new plan. Just as he's doing that, a great big . . . O gosh it's noisy, built real low to the ground,

real nice and sleek, you know, one of them foreign sports cars . . .
I don't know the name of it or nothing . . . but sitting behind the
wheel there's a woman – you would've thought that god had
designed her to drive every last s.o.b. on earth absolutely stark
raving mad. She rolls over and cranks down the window, and gives
him a great big smile that'd drive any fellow right round the bend.
She says,

"Where you going?"

"I was just going in to the Five Corners to exercise my
franchise," the old fellow says. "Awful good of you to stop."

"O," she says, "my gosh, come on get in. Who you voting for?"

"Well," he stops for a second or two, pauses a little bit, you
know. Then says, "Liberals."

"O," she says. "Get in."

He clambers in. Gosh, the car smells, you know, the way new
cars do, leather. Like John Wayne'd say, smells all over like a
woman. Well, he sits there, proud as punch, grinning from ear to
ear, and just looking like a jackass. They's driving along, she don't
say nothing to him, he don't say nothing to her. After about, O
maybe five minutes, she looks over at where he's sitting and says,

"You know, you ain't said nothing yet. What you sitting there
thinking about?"

"I was wondering what you was thinking about," he says.

"Come on now, I asked you first," she says.

"Well," he says, "Funny thing you're asking me. I was sitting
here thinking I've only been a Liberal for five minutes and already
I wanna screw somebody." ●

2
The
Golden Age of
Restraint

You know by now who I'm talking about – the holy order of the
Liberal Party. In some ways you gotta admire them ginks. They've
refined the gimmicks of showbusiness to a pretty fine point. O sure.
Showbusiness. You bet. I'm in showbusiness, and nowadays, just
about everyone else is in showbusiness too; it don't matter who
you're talking about, it can be the queen of England, or the pope.
As a matter of fact, it wasn't too long ago I was on a speaking
engagement, and we was having questions from the floor, and a
fellow puts his hand up and he says, "Fred, what do you think
about this story going around that the pope's a fruit?" And I says
that's what happens to you when you're in showbusiness, people'll
say just about anything.

Anyways, if anyone was ever in showbusiness, in Canada, and
don't you forget it, it's a bird by the name of Pierre Elliott

Trudeau. And, of course, I'm in showbusiness too. In fact, I started out in Port Matoon. That's spelled M-o-u-t-o-n – French. And it's pronounced Matoon. Course some guys in the CBC, putting on the dog, called it Port Moo-tone. Course, no one knew what the hell they was talking about. Anyways, I go right back to the days when you could work across Canada, go slick and clean across the country to Spuzzum, British Columbia. Geez, in them days, we used to go down the Pacific Coast – Washington state, Oregon, into California where I once acted in a John Wayne motion picture. Played a dead Japanese – too tall for a live one.

Anyways, to cut the cackle, the Liberal Party of Canada was having a fund-raising dinner at the Four Seasons Sheraton Hotel, and the guest speaker, or the guest of honor, don't matter much, was none other than Trudeau himself. I should mention that for this august, historic moment of theatre, Trudeau was wearing only two of his hats; one was the cap of the leader of the Liberal Party, and the other was the top hat of the prime minister of Canada. He did not bother with his "Great Canadian" hat, although you might have thought that he was wearing it, too. In years to come his government will surely make millions of tax dollars available to thirty groups of three, (always professors), to write – in French and English, mind – the *Tales of Pierre Elliot Trudeau*, unexpurgated and suitable for hand delivery in plain brown wrappers. There won't be no mail or post office, cause the whole thing will have collapsed under the weight of its giant stamp collections. So, if it ain't happened already, if you write a letter, then you'll have to deliver the sucker yourself. There'll be no delivery. That's right. There will be no mail delivery as we know it nowadays. That'll go out like Wells Fargo with its wagons and teams. But there'll be stamps. O, by the blue geez, there will be enough stamps for every Canadian to put a hundred of the blamed things on his arse any day of the week. All kindsa stamps. And you better not try and make your own delivery without a stamp, because if you do, you'll be in serious trouble.

Canadians will smile, with sad eyes, looking at their old red letter boxes on display in various Information Canada museums. Mind you, there will be no "royal" mail boxes on display. Just the

Canada mail ones, cause you must remember when you got more solutions, more ideas, and more slogans than the *Holy Bible*, you can pretty well go into history, whatever way you want. Not to knock the *Bible*, because they was a pretty slick buncha fellows. As I said, they was the birds that would come up with the slogans like, "The Meek Shall Inherit the Earth." Ain't no ad agency in the world that's ever topped that one! When they cooked up that one, maybe *that's* when we should have unfurled the bullshit banner. We'll give them credit. Not one of our modern-day backroom toadies could ever match that one. The meek shall inherit the earth. Ain't that a dilly?

Speaking of the post office, there was some good news on the subject. Don't know whether you caught it or not, but the Polish and the Canadian governments merged, as far as the post office set-up is concerned. That was the good news. The bad news was, the Canadians was gonna run it.

Anyways, in the spring of 1975, there he was, Trudeau himself, the man for the Liberal's big one-hundred-dollar-a-plate dinner, and guess what his theme was? Restraint! Yeah, that's right, *restraint*. Now, ain't that wicked? Here they're all having themselves a time in the Four Seasons Sheraton. You'd think they'd have staged her in a McDonald's at least, but O no, not that outfit. They don't have to worry none about their plastered-on power cracking. Restraint, even with Trudeau, at a hundred dollars a plate. How about that nice little ripoff? They'd have to say it was a Royal Ripoff, or how about *Ripoff Royale*. It sounds like a fast toilet paper, don't it? And in the middle of this fabulous fund-raiser, the politicians was wrestling with the biggest daily double since Adam was a little baby. What am I talking about? Well, I'm talking about the million dollar deal each federal member of parliament gets in his sixties, providing he's kept himself in office by hook or by crook for ten years. Not bad, eh? Salary and pensions after ten years adds up to about a million in your sixties.

Now, these are the same very people that got welfare for their friends at Syncrude, but give them credit. They did run through a few pennies for the old sweats . . . senior citizens they call us. Ain't that wonderful? Did you ever hear of a more jackass title than that in your life? Anytime anyone puts that title on me I just say, "Well listen, Junior Citizen, you know who you're talking to?" And think about all the poor old souls that laid their lives on the line, back in them days when you done it for your king . . . and I ain't talking about Mackenzie . . . and country. Can you imagine being up to your fanny in mud somewhere in France in World War I, getting shot at, then catching one, but somehow surviving, then spending four or five decades fighting veterans affairs, health and welfare, and finally your own flesh and blood? And there *he* was, preaching restraint. There's just no two ways about it, that had to be, as far as I was concerned, the threshold of the golden age of bullshit. Nowadays, it just ain't a question of governments daring to cheat the eyes out of the people's heads. They ain't daring. No, it's all gotten beyond that, because for them there's no risk whatsoever. The only real danger nowadays, might be the boredom riots. That's right. Boredom riots could break out, but where or when it's just hard to say. Maybe all them suckers that come over to Loblaws . . . can't you see it, fifty-seven shoppers lined up at the express counters start shouting, "The price is *not* right!" All of a sudden there, Bill Shatner comes in and he winks and they kill him! That's right, they kill him right there on the spot! Just as he clenches his fist and looks into the camera to bullshit you one more time – By Gosh, the Price Is Right – the old ladies rush out and club him down with their cans of Javex. Imagine someone driving a jolly-green-giant bean right up his arse. Ain't that wicked?

Seriously, though, it's not hard to predict that there'll be some kinda rebellion. Remember Boston. They didn't have the guts to come right up front with it, and toss the tea in the harbor. No, they had to go and put on a whole lotta makeup and feathers. You know, it's a wonderful thing; businessmen never call one another fruits for dressing up. And you'll see them all over the world with paper hats and water pistols, and motorcycles, but they'll look down on actors anytime of the year. It's another part of their double standards. Anyways, they tossed the tea into the harbor, and good old George III shit himself, and that was the end of that. England never knew when they had it so good. They sure blew that one. In our day it won't be tea from England. She'll be pot from Asia, and not teapot either. Maybe senior citizens will run amock at Vancouver International Airport wrecking the pot planes. Can't you see it? A buncha old sweats, their trusses lashed on, rushing out onto the tanbark, and tearing the pot right outa the 747 bellies.

Remember the days when they said the country couldn't afford a $300 million national medicare program? Remember that? When they give us that? The same lying government has just jammed a billion plus airport up our fanny which everyone says is a national disaster. The same ginks gave us a billion plus Olympiad. If you're a crook in structural steel and cement in Montreal, who worked on the Olympics on a no-bid contract deal, geez, you'd better have your goddamned hotel booked in Marakech because they'll be on your arse. You've had the word from the premier – the people of Quebec will love it! They'll love it. They love it being stuck right in and broke off. They get a kick out of it. You know, it's a funny thing about criticizing this system. When you do it, and you get close to the bone, it don't matter if it's the Shouldice Surgery Old Boy's Association, the Canadian Tobacco Dealers, or Canada Dildo – it don't matter who's gathering together to beat their breast and feel a little expansive and lay a medal on someone for better sales, or whatever. Geez, as soon as you start talking about the system, you're threatening them. You're coming close to the bone. The thing that I've noticed is that the system gets its protection from the very people that's being screwed by it. They're the ones that go right on in the battle for it, every time. And they say, "O geez, Fred, Loblaws is a pretty good firm. Two point seven billion in 74. They employ a lotta people." That's parta the bullshit nowadays. "Business is in business for the purpose of employing people." You know that there's an awful lotta firms that have been hiding behind *that* bullshit. The government encourages the people to think, "Business is in business to give out jobs." That's why the old-fashioned thing – "We're in business to make a profit, to make a buck" – nothing wrong with that. Just come forward and say it. But no, they're all kinda cooking things, that we musn't let this thing collapse. We can't let that goal be beat. Jobs will be lost – jobs, it's all jobs. That's parta the golden age of bullshit.

Where was I? I kinda went round Cape Horn again. I took off on that for a second.

Let's see now, remember them days when the country couldn't afford a $300 million medicare program. Now we can afford million dollar payoffs for people who make a career outa politics in Ottawa, providing they get in for ten consecutive years. We can afford that. O yes. We can afford thousands of words, thousands of man-hours on, "Should John Bassett Junior be allowed to have an American football franchise in the city of Toronto?" We can afford to have hundreds of Ontario Tories on the phone, writing letters, going to see people to lay down as much influence as they can to help poor little Johnny Junior with his football scheme. But can we afford to kick in say, eighty bucks, for a destitute family? No! Ontario is the proof of the pudding that now, after three years of bullshitting, they can't even come up with as much concrete information on the subject as Prince Edward Island. No way. *No way.*

People say, "Well, Fred, what are you talking about? Are you trying to bust the taxpayer down another eighty bucks for someone who can't even . . . I'm talking about the working poor. I'm talking about people who get up off their arse, don't want a handout, don't want to be on welfare, don't want unemployment insurance. They do rotten little jobs as paid slaves. They try and hold their end of the stick up, and it's obvious they need a little bit of supplement for their income. And all the business bastards of the country run around saying, "Geez, we don't want that. It's socialism." But they sure love socialism for business. They love socialism for the rich. They love having socialism for Syncrude – socialism for General Motors in Oshawa. They love socialism for themselves. The Bank of Commerce and Labatts breweries love socialism for the expansion of the Canadian National Exhibition grandstand. They love socialism to the tune of $15 million to put 15,000 seats in. *That's* socialism when the people of Toronto have to kick that money in, so the middle class can sit down there and watch the biggest restrainters in the history of professional football play their goddamn game. There's no one in this country that's practised restraint like the Toronto Argonauts.

Socialism for the rich. Ask Nixon about it. Ask the United States government about it. Private, with a capital P, firms that lived off the taxpayers of the United States to the tune of billions and billions of dollars. And these same goddamn people run around all the time talking about, "Geez, we don't want socialism for the poor, we don't want handouts for this outfit, or handouts for that." They love handouts for themselves though. Socialism is a word that's kinda disappeared. It's kinda like capitalism. After the crash, capitalism disappeared. The word that replaced it was free enterprise. Free enterprise is when Loblaws puts twenty-two hundred items on the shelf and then boasts publicly that all twenty-two hundred sell for the same amount of money as their rivals. *That's* the great paragons of free enterprise at work. Free enterprise is when the banks of Canada, within seventy-two hours, all announce exactly the same interest rates. Free enterprise in Canada is when it costs the same amount of money to send a telegram whether you use CP or CN. By the way, there's no way those suckers will get off their arses, mount a bicycle, and go deliver it. They'll phone it. And if you're not home, tough ass, it will come in the mail a year later. That's the golden age of bullshit.

And what I like, is when people get their wind up and say, "He's going too strong. He's driving too hard. He's got the whip out. I don't want to hear it. It hurts." They're the very fellows I aim it at, and they're the ones who *do* need the crack on the head, because they like to put it any other way than it really is. They are the bullshitters. They are the guys that never say the price is *lower*. So don't tell me how the golden age of bullshit goes along. It goes along every single day in the lives of *every* Canadian.

People used to say to me, "Fred, why don't you get a platform yourself, and go into politics? Stop beating your gums and stand on the soapbox. Why don't you take part?" It's like old Bob Stanfield, the poor old gink. If he stood sideways we'd have to mark him absent. He was lamenting the fact that democracy seems to be threatened in Canada, because Canadians don't have a good opinion of politicians and politics. He was lamenting the fact that Canadians don't go actively into politics no more, especially the young people. What they do, he says, is, they band together in citizen organizations. They mount pressure groups.

Well, I don't know where Stanfield's been, but we've already been having the rise of pressure groups, and we're now living through the fall of them. Half of them don't even draw flies no more. The politicians have ridden them out. They've ridden them out real good. A lot of them's cashed in. The mayor of Toronto, he saw high-pressure groups didn't want high buildings. He's still in office. Why? Because he stuck in a forty-five foot restriction law. Done real good. You have to worry about protecting the neighborhood. He might have meant it. How do I know if he did or not? He got in on it. He used it real good.

Here, now, is Stanfield, saying how sorry and upset he is. Canadians is looking out the window while their democracy is going the other way. Now isn't it a funny thing that we have a bad opinion of politics and politicians? Should we have any other kind of opinion of them? Do we really think they're wonderful? And you can sit in Canada and talk to any cabinet minister or any member of Canada's parliamentary family, and what's the first thing they're going to do? They're going to sit there, with that big chip on their shoulder, and tell you how misunderstood they is. And how grim it is, and how no one really knows just how tough and rough the whole situation is, because they're out there on the parapets saving us from the great evil tide of something else. But it's all in their minds, as far as I'm concerned.

Now, take an example. Did an elected representative or official in the United States in any concrete way put an end to the Vietnam war? *No.* Pressure groups. Students. Students banding together. They brought the hatred of the adults out. That's when the mask was tore off America – supposedly the country that worships youth and loves it. They're *terrified* of youth. They hate the sight of them. They're jealous of them. These old senators who can't get it up any more, they can't stand the thought of these kids running around in four-dollar suits, which in effect say, "Screw you, I like my blue jeans! I'm not dressing up in your Hart, Schaffner & Marx outfit." They're terrified. Darn right. No, it was pressure groups drove Johnson outa office. And sure as hell didn't give Tricky Dick a good time either. That war was stopped by public pressure. And the pressure got so good that even United States business, and you don't have to be a Commie to come on with this line either, when United States business started leaning on Washington saying, "enough is enough, we can't afford it." It's bad-sport time. I've never seen it fail. Worst sports in the world. They can't win it, then it's no good. Well, they seen they couldn't win it. They found out they couldn't win it. It's like the Russians in World War I. The Russian army wasn't worth a goddamn in World War I. They didn't wanna fight for the Czar and the right of some nobleman to try his pistols out on some slaves working out in the fields. So they didn't. So the US couldn't win that thing out in Vietnam because there wasn't the will to win it. They didn't want to go all the way and be big bullies in the eyes of everyone in the world and do the bomb on them. They didn't want to live with that one.

Now, we'll take another example. Name me an elected representative or some guy in government that's been big for the consumer in North America. Name me some anti-trust organization that's really gone out for the public. *No one.* But Ralph Nader, an outside man leading pressure groups, he's really done something for the public. So that's my answer to the Stanfields of this world that hide behind this big cloak of respectability, lamenting that Canadians, they ain't interested in Canadian politics no more. I say it shows the intelligence of people nowadays, if they just ain't gonna go along with the bullshit that's being cranked out. That, to me, is a good sign. And I think that it's a wonderful thing that we don't all assemble together in a parking lot and shout our heads off and look like a bunch of jackasses when we see our leader. We have a few examples in this century of what happened to the country and the rest of the countries around them, with people who had that kind of adulation up their sleeve for someone who supposedly had all the answers. Starting off with unemployment and "Strength Through Joy," and you name it.

I mind the time when I thought the answer *was* politics, and I thought I'd run for mayor. By geez, I didn't have much of a platform but I promised to let the air outa some people's rubbers. First thing, I thought I was gonna do, was to stop old Eaton's,

Canada's largest finance company from grabbing old Santa by the bag and rushing him down Yonge Street on Labor Day. And no more of that, "While Shepherds Wash Their Socks at Night" stuff, round bout Hallowe'en. Who the hell wants to hear that? As a matter of fact, I wouldn't mind putting on a "Let's Put Christ Back into Christmas" march, just to put the bastards in their place. Anyways, I really found out that most people kinda like to have the old marketplace reaching out and grabbing them by the bag. They don't mind going stony broke. When the boredom riots break out we'll smell the stench of burning plastic. One of the first things to go will be the credit card.

Now to return to the age of bullshit, let's concentrate on the provincials. Take Ontari-ari-ario. The reigning monarch for quite a while now has been King Billy Davis. He's gotta little nervous about people getting riled up about too much government spending. So, better give the people some sorta safeguard. Get the idea? A safeguard over their money. In a pig's whisper. O boys, so what do they do? They create an ombudsman. Ain't that wonderful? In the golden age of bullshit you do anything and everything. It's kinda like what the New Deal boys put across to the US in the 1930s. In the main, it was designed to forestall the inevitable. That's what it really was all about. And you know, if you talk to some good, old, hard-line socialists, they'll tell you that World War I was designed to stop socialism. Now that ought to stick in the throats of a few people. So if you're hot now, put your flashlight out and get your hands outside the covers.

Anyways, the idea is, your ombudsman will scrutinize your government. Already you got your government cabinet empowered to scrutinize government spending. The province of Ontario just don't leave it to a cabinet. No sir. There's also an outfit called a management board to scrutinize government spending. Then, there's what they call departmental estimates. It can also scrutinize government spending. O yes. And when you're talking about the legislature, you gotta be talking about your MPPs as well. You know what I mean? Some of them MPPs sit on things like the public accounts committee. And *them* birds, is all empowered, *every one of them* I've named, every last sonofabitching one of them, to scrutinize government spending.

To go on, there's a bird called the provincial auditor. Talk about low profiles. Anyone remember him? He's empowered to scrutinize government spending. So how many people do we want to name? I'm giving you the facts. You can run to any library you want, or any politician who knows all his politics from A to Z, and he won't be able to add anything to the list I've given you, but he won't be able to tear anything out of it either. Because, I'm telling you, all the people that's empowered to look into government spending. No less than *five* ways government spending can be, and should be scrutinized. Now in the age of bullshit, we've got to have a *sixth* way. A *simple*, easy way. That's a wonderful commercial word, easy. They always hire some guy who sounds like he's got a set of basketballs between his knees, to say it on the radio – *EASY* – you know what I mean?

The ombudsman, he's the easy way to sum it all up. You've got him running around then by geez, you've really done something. It's all grandstanding. I've seen the ombudsman himself right on the TV talking about how he didn't have enough money to run his office. Ain't that fantastic? Here we set up a sixth device to protect the poor old paid slaves who are supporting the whole leprous apparatus, and there he is right on TV telling us that he don't have enough money. He can't get enough money out of the government to do the job. Why geez, they call themselves grown-up, civilized, sensible – and as soon as you start yapping at them, barking at them, you become the enemy. You show a fellow that you know more than he does, and show him at the same time that you know he's bullshitting you, and he'll hate your guts. Did you ever see it fail? You can have a relationship with anyone anywhere, but don't ever let a guy that's trying to pull the wool over your eyes, know that you know he's doing it, because he'll hate you. It's the same with the government. To hell with them yapping about scrutinizing. Why don't they scrap scrutinizing and say screwing? After all, government spending means money for the public – you see, it is *our* money, not theirs. They *do* work for us; we *don't* work for them.

We're awful kind in Canada to governments and civil services.

It's too bad they ain't too kind to us. It's like the guy that says to me the other day, he says, "There's an awful lot of people on government payrolls." I says, "O geez, I know there is." He says, "Well how many do you think? How many do you think's working for the government now?" "I don't know," says I. He says, "About half."

Then he says to me, he says, "Fred, how can you tell when a civil servant winks?" I says, "When a civil servant winks?" He says, "Yes." I says, "I don't know." He says, "When he opens one eye."

Anyways, since we've just let a little air out of some federal and provincial rubbers, let's not forget the municipal boys. Take urban planning. That's when they promise you the Garden of Eden and give you Buffalo instead. Or they wage an all-out propaganda campaign against the city's massage parlors.

Geez, you know I wish I could say I was just like an old toilet seat, born and raised in Barrie, Ontario, but Beamsville's my town. Now, Beamsville's where an old Jacob Beam, United Empire Loyalist guy, back in the time of old Governor Simcoe, first settled. Before the golden age of bullshit. Beamsville had to suffer neighbors in Grimsby gladly, cause Grimsby had a liquor store and Beamsville didn't. Mind you, Beamsville had liquor and wine too. Many's the time I sat in old Busby's variety store and split the shoulders of a bottle of Derby.

Them was the days. Had a tiny dirt farm. Nothing fancy. Just a couple of acres. That's where old Robarts, my dog, could run real free, and sometimes he would get the old mare – Duddie's Adios – all stirred up. Geez, that'd be fun. She was in her late twenties then, but she could trot pretty good. I tried to breed her every year, but, as they say in the racing game, we never got nothing to take. Just couldn't get her into foal no matter what we tried. But I'll tell you one thing: she sure loved to play the game. Grew a little Seneca Chief corn, out there, and some tomatoes, ones with real taste, not like them ones from Mexico and California they flog in the winter. And a little pot too, a little cannabis. That was all back in the good old days when a fellow could register Mr. and Mrs. at the old Ford Hotel in Toronto, at the corner of Bay and Dundas Streets, right in the soft underbelly of the city, and go to the room with a monkey on his arm. No one would bat an eye. All you done, was put down your two-fifty for the room and a dollar for the key. The Ford Hotel. The old Bay Street riding academy.

She's gone now, but at least the management had the decency to train its clerks to never ask no one for identification. Mind you, they was real quick in asking for $2.50 in advance. She was real close to the old Bowles lunch just down the way from the site of the old Ford, where Bay Street twists across Queen. Across from the new City Hall now stands the Four Seasons Sheraton Hotel. This is, of course, where Trudeau preached his great sermon on restraint, at the $100-a-plate dinner of the Liberal Party fund-raising dinner. All of this in the midst of fast-moving action to bring in the largest bonanza that elected or non-elected representation in the history of western world politics has ever known. There ain't a business in Canada that could afford the pension scheme we've now got for our federal mandarins and our elected representatives. Not a business in the country. Not even Imperial Oil. Mind you, they're not so big. They started selling out to Rockerfeller in 1899. That's another great Canadian story, with an ending as good as the *Bluenose*. I hear they got to ask New Jersey for permission to write a cheque for five million. Well, you know what they say: About five percent of your people's interested in politics, but about a hundred percent gets screwed by it. ●

3
You Can't Buy the Truth for Fifteen cents

In the golden age of bullshit, the one thing that's got to stick out is the role of what they nowadays call the media. The "media," of course, is just one of them words brought over the border by things like the Holy Order of the Liberal Party of Canada, Canadian universities, the campus middle-classers. Old Yankee doodle jargon. What we're talking about is, first and foremost, the newspapers, and the wire services and, of course, the TV and radio. I mention the TV and the radio last, not so much because they oughta be there cause when the facts is all in, most folks sit glued to the TV a lot more than they do with a newspaper. If anyone was guilty of tailgating anyone, riding on the coattails of anyone, it's the TV and the radio . . . O, they're tailgating the newspapers most of the time. I have to say that the CBC national news, which is an institution in this country . . . geez, there's been more Canadians gone to bed with Earl Cameron and Lloyd Robertson than Carter's got little liver pills . . . there's just no way The National can be put out without what they call the bulldog edition of the *Globe and Mail*. That's the first edition of the *Globe and Mail* to hit the streets around nine o'clock at night. There's no way the CBC boys, controlled by United States unions, would ever get anything out on to the sheet for old Lloyd to read without first scanning the old *Globe*. That's where they get most of their news, their inspirations. If it's in print, then it's official, you get the idea?

I mind the time I was in Winnipeg, and by geez, a story come out there . . . a couple of private detectives was propositioning a bunch of denturists, the fellows that make cheap clackers; in other words, they cut the middle chisler out. Now, under the old Dental Act of Manitoba, which is a real democratic piece of legislation since it's policed by the dentists themselves, the only way they can get evidence about illegalities in the field of dentistry – in other words, competition that's cheaper than the kind of locked-up, gun-to-the-head the dentists've been using – is to get private detectives to go out and act as *agents provocateurs* and get evidence. So these two detectives go to five denturists at a dental laboratory and they says, "Now you deliver us a couple of patsies and we'll slap fines on them, and that way the dentists of Manitoba will be happy." You get the idea? "Cause under the act," these detectives say, "that'll mean we've delivered the goods on a couple of guys violating the dental act."

Well, it just so happened that these five denturists wasn't so half-witted as the detectives was, cause they taped the whole proceedings. And they took the tape, through their representative, spokesman name of Gordon Smith who'd done a big job for the denturists, and for anyone wanting cheap clackers he's got to go down as a national hero. As a matter of fact, he should have a Canada Medal. But there ain't no way that people like that get Canada Medals. If they're gonna give out a Canada Medal they look up the Archbishop of Rimouski and hang another one round his dong. Here's what I'm coming to, and this is real important: it kinda shows you where the TV boys is at when it comes to news.

This fellow, Gordon Smith, is a real hustler for the denturists, putting their case forward, sends the tape into CBWT, Winnipeg, the flagship of the CBC prairie region. Now, do you think there was any way the CBC news in Winnipeg would carry the story of these two private detectives propositioning five denturists with a plan to deliver two patsies to the dentists? *No*, geez, they said, "If that ain't in the *Free Press* or the *Tribune* we won't touch it." That's what they actually said: That's the god's honest truth. Well, the public-affairs guys, not knowing any better, put it on the air, held the tape up, interviewed the five denturists, told the story. Then, the *Tribune*, then the *Free Press*, carried the story. By geez, the attorney general of Manitoba, the head of the dental association, the head of the Winnipeg police, Chief George Blow, they *all* wanted in on it, they all wanted transcripts. By geez, charges was laid against the two private detectives. Then, and not until then, did the CBC Winnipeg news finally carry the story – it was in print, you get the idea?

So, I just kinda wanted to get that in focus. We're talking about the golden age of bullshit, so let's get all the bullshit vendors in focus, and understand who we're dealing with, let's understand just how rough and tough these boys really is.

Now, the CBC Winnipeg news boys wouldn't carry the story until it appeared in the papers even though it had been carried on the CBC by the public-affairs boys. Then the CBC news, the divine queen of battle, went into action and tailgated the whole story that was right in front of them in the *Free Press* and the *Tribune*. Now, there's no other way I can lay it in than that. Them's the facts. When did it happen? The winter of 1965-6, a well-known story.

You remember the time . . . by geez, what an awful time it was . . . when they reported that President John Kennedy had been shot by an assassin in Dallas, Texas? That was the first bulletin. The next one, in that awful month of November, 1963, the next bulletin was that there was no conspiracy. A bunch of people who had no facts at their disposal rushed into print and went on the TV and radio . . . sheriffs and god knows what all . . . to tell the American people there was no conspiracy. That was awful important, to lay that in within twenty-four hours despite the fact that they'd investigated sweet buggerall.

Now, at the time this news was flashing around the world, before Kennedy was actually declared dead in the Parkland Hospital in Dallas, by the doctors there . . . that, of course was before the bungled autopsy that took place in Washington . . . Bill Cunningham, who's now running the Global TV news, goes to a CBC executive who's controlling the purse strings for the CBC news up here in Toronto where everything's supposed to be wonderful, and says,

"There's a big story in Dallas, Texas, someone shot the president of the United States, we're getting a crew together to go down there and we gotta have money, and we gotta have plane tickets, we gotta get with it."

The CBC executive says – now, believe it not, this is what the man says . . . mind you he had a great background for the job: he was a corporal in the British army in Greece . . . he says,

"The story of the president of the United States being shot by an assassin is of no interest to the Canadian people."

Now, that is a CBC news biggie . . . now there you are . . . I mean the golden age . . . no *wonder* there's bullshit in Canada; look at the powers that be, look at the intermediate, lickspittle, toady, jackasses that's running around with their fingers on the levers of power. No wonder people like Trudeau can go from coast to coast spreading his own brand of bullshit when he knows he's got people like this all over the country.

I get a great kick out of mentioning that one. That is my all-time CBC story. I love it, I *love* it. Cause they get over $300 million a year, they got over 9,000 people and all they can do is pump up two shows in the top thirty – you know, the "Olympic Lottery" show and "Hockey Night in Canada." The other twenty-eight's made elsewhere. Geez, I got off the track there. Where the hell was I?

We're talking about the media, the newspapers, the TV, and the radio boys and their contribution to the golden age of B. S. Well actually, they're the linchpin, when you get right down to it, they're the linchpin of the whole deal. When you figure out the number of papers that are published in Canada in one day and you multiply it by the number of pages . . . geez it's fantastic. Take the *Toronto Star*, I don't know how many pages she's got but you take out the supermarket ads, and the real estate ads, and the car ads, she's down to about eight minutes of reading. Otherwise, think of the number of trees that has to be felled on a daily basis to put that sucker out and all cause the boss of the thing, Beland Honderich, wants nice little stories so that everyone thinks there's a silver lining and a wonderful carrot in fronta each donkey that goes galloping around the field. That way no one'll be upset and they'll keep on coming up with their fifteen cents for the truth. Now you know, you just *know*, you ain't gonna buy the truth for fifteen cents. If you want to give credit where credit's due, consider the *Daily Racing Form*. Now *there's* a paper, reporting everything there is to know on every horse that's racing, from the standpoint of the horses' class, consistency, weight, form, speed – all sortsa other facts and figures and pieces of information. Aside from the *Form* there's probably the *Wall Street Journal* and the *Christian Science Monitor* and that's it. And if people say, "O, come on Fred, that's not fair," as I'm sure someone like Charlie Lynch might say, between mouth-organ concerts for the prime minister, let's put it this way: 2,000 reporters in Washington, DC, at the time of Watergate and less than five was working on the Watergate story. That gives you an idea of the press – we're no different in Canada.

Here's a little tale that'll put the thing more in focus than anything else.

Way back, a million years ago it seems, in the city of Vancouver, a fellow by the name of Ray Munro, an RCAF hero in World War II, a fellow who's got all kind of world records in balloon flying, he goes to both Vancouver dailies with a story about the worst scandal god ever told the other fellow about, concerning corruption in the Vancouver city police department. Well, the two papers being real paragons of free enterprise and upholders of the truth and believers of all that's fit to be printed (or whatever the saying is), they turned him down flat. There was no way they wanted any part of it.

Now, Munro does all this leg work on the corruption on the Vancouver city police force. He can't get neither paper to rise to the bait. Won't touch it with a barge pole. So Munro goes to old Lou Ruby down in Toronto and he's got a paper called *Flash Weekly*. If you're in the upper 400, there's just no way in the world you're going to advertise the fact that you read it. O, all kindsa people's buying it, they're putting it in the middle part of a *Time* magazine, they don't want to be seen reading it. Well, when the *Flash* come out in Vancouver with the story on the Vancouver policy that Munro wrote and the two chickenshit papers of the city wouldn't print, that paper sold out slicker'n . . . well just like its name. Geez, in minutes that edition of *Flash* just disappeared from the streets. They named names . . . boys O boys, did he ever have the goods on them. And I'm telling you, everyone got their shorts in a knot in a pretty quick time.

There was lot of horrible, sad repercussions to the tale, too. First of all, one policeman committed suicide, another bungled the attempt to bump himself off and a certain police official puts in an application for a visa to the United States of America, and *un*like most Canadians gets a visa in *three days flat.* You, me, when we apply for a visa it takes the government maybe two-three months to clear it. Sure. Geez, they takes your fingerprints, send them to the FBI, check your references in the US of A, put you through hoops, is what they do. Don't tell us in Canada, in the golden age of bullshit, let's not nobody try to get that old fogey over of "everyone's equal under the law." Let's face it, there's laws for the rich and there are other laws for those of us who ain't got the wampum.

Geez, there was an attempt at this time on Munro's life, you know. One night he was walking across the Granville Street bridge and a couple Hoosiers brought in from Oregon state tried to toss him over the side there, but he handled himself pretty good much to the displeasure of one of the Hoosiers. He ruffled a lot of feathers, old Munro did.

Incidentally it was his covering of the corruption in the Vancouver police force that put old Jack Webster on the map. He was the reporter for CJOR radio and he had a show called "City Mike." By geez, he'd stand on the Vancouver city courthouse steps at the corner of Robson and Howe Streets, and he'd do a live radio report that'd just chill the cocktails of your heart. Boys O boys, he'd be fresh out of court with the latest stuff that had been going on, and he'd be talking over all the evidence that was in up to that point. Every day they had a live broadcast of what was going on. Matter of fact, Webster made his name covering this whole thing, all these shenanigans, and geez, he done a hell of a job, I'm telling you. If private radio ever wants to stand up once in a while in the broadcasting sea of turds and fly a battle flag it's gotta be with the likes of Jack Webster cause, like they say it nowadays, he told it like it was. Webster used to do the horseraces too, with old Jack Shortt, right at the track. But, that's kinda going around Cape Horn there.

Another one of the stories that came out of the case concerned one of the sharpest detectives that ever plied his trade in the city of Vancouver. That was a fellow, known as, well let's call him officer ABC. Fact is, the boys on the force used to say that if you want to catch a thief, you hire a thief and that's why this detective was on the force. I'll tell you he didn't take a backseat to no one. The Province of British Columbia, in its case against the Vancouver police, can you imagine this in the courts, can you imagine what a fantastic preoccupation this would've been with everyone? This story was so big in the city of Vancouver that people even forgot about the city's top abortionist, just for once, and they even forgot about the fact there wasn't going to be a new Marpole bridge. They actually bore down on the fact that here and there was a few greasy dollars changing hands in their own wonderful city of Vancouver. *Yeah.* Anyways . . .

The crown said they was going to introduce as evidence a certain photograph they had in their possession which showed this Vancouver detective sitting in the grandstand box of one Joey Perhaps at the Bay Meadows racetrack, down near San Francisco. Now, one might say, "What the hell's the matter with that?" Here's a Vancouver police officer on his holidays, or whatever, sitting with Joey Perhaps, a Vancouver citizen. The only trouble is that Perhaps was well-known in Vancouver, in and out of the press, as one of the city's leading bookmakers. So the crown thought that was pretty good to have a picture of one of the city's well-known police officers on his holidays sitting with one of the city's top bookmakers. You get the picture?

"Well," the police said, "that sounds pretty good. Only thing is, we got a certain photograph, too, you guys. You might be interested in knowing what *it* shows." This, of course, is all in the back rooms, you know, this ain't coming out in the court, this is behind the scenes. You get the idea? This is where some of the real rough stuff goes on. So the crown says, "What's your picture?"

Well they come right to the point. The cops ain't fools you know, you gotta get up pretty early in the morning to beat them, you know, in spite of the fact that most of them ain't too swift. The cops say, "Listen. We gotta picture of a certain politician of the province of British Columbia, holding a girl by the ankles, she's standing on her hands, she ain't got nothing – *nothing* – on. There's some other bird there with a spoon that's got an egg on it, holding it right over the key station of her network. So, how you think that's gonna look, we let that picture out to the press?"

Are the good god-fearing people of Vancouver who read the *Reader's Digest,* who wait up at night to hear Earl Cameron, and believe in the dynasty of Mackenzie King and Louis St. Laurent and Lester Pearson, really gonna swallow that? Are they really gonna feel happy about that one?

So, needless to say, the picture of the police officer and the bookmaker kinda faded into the doldrums. Once again, clear proof of the fact that the biggies of this world protect their arse once they're up there. (Geez, now that I come to think of it, maybe it was the politician who held the spoon and the egg. I don't rightly remember but there was no doubt about the key station of the girl's network. O no! The picture was very explicit.)

I told how one police officer managed to get out of town, landed immigrant's status in US of A in three days. You know, there's one thing about the government of Canada; when you put the boots to it and say, "This is a special, – a three-star special. Get on with it!" they can drop everything and actually function. They can launch a rocket if you tell them to. No way they can drag their arse when they get the message that this is something Big with a capital B. O, they know how to move. O yeah. But they're not gonna bust their balls for you if you're just Joe McDoaks lining up for a visa; you'll wait your bloody turn.

And of course, the real estate outfits, the car makers, and the supermarkets fill the pages of the newspapers with junk every week. It's fair to say no newspaper's going to tromp all over them at any time. They're going to bury any teensy weensy little story that might frighten them birds. We got a housing shortage; it *is* a national scandal, it *is* a terrible disgrace. Has anyone gone to work on it at any newspaper in Canada? Has anyone put together the whole thing? Has anyone investigated the mechanics of it? Have they lamented the fact that we've got all kinds of labor available, all kinds of material, all kinds of capital that should be put to use? *No!* They've not said a damned thing; they've just sat and run the ads, and had their hands out, jerked off with everybody. Meanwhile, we've had the unmitigated gall and nerve to host an international housing conference in the City of Vancouver calling it Habitat. What a joke! It's almost like South Africa claiming they got a diamond shortage. Well, they *do* have a diamond shortage, that's the whole point of diamonds. There's enough diamonds to cover everyone's arse in the world, we could run around with our arse ringed in diamonds, but they've created a shortage. Right? That's why they search everyone who comes out of the mines, they look up his arse to see if he's got one spirited away there. Cause they wanna make absolutely sure they know where every one is. Same with the houses in Canada.

The guys that control all the B.S., they know *exactly* what they're doing. The old idea of a young couple having a home of their own now is a thing of the past. That's as ridiculous as going on a world cruise, for god's sake. It's gone out with the dodo. That's a careful, calculated business scam foisted on the people of Canada. Canadians don't know which way was up. They should get out of here and get down to the United States and go to some place like Florida, and see forty-fifty thousand dollar houses available with *nothing* down – get that fellows? – nothing down! No seedy, crappy, gummy, little government subsidy . . . nothing down *and* a six percent mortgage. Try and get a six percent mortgage in Canada. Yeah. *O* yeah! You can mark that one up on ice.

It's terrific. It's part of our golden age. Now, when I'm on the rubber-chicken circuit, I *love* sending out salvos to the divine right of the middle-class boys, who sit there assembled, full of booze, their bladders bulging, with some rotten rubber chicken in their gut. But they sit there and say, "This s.o.b. who's speaking to us right at this minute, ain't telling us what we want to hear. He ain't conning us. We're used to being conned." *That's* the definition of a con man: a con man's a fellow tells you what you wanna hear. "He ain't conning us." They're sensitive to that cause they're con men, they know how to con people more than do the men with the licenses on the wall. That's their whole bloody game. Suddenly they hear someone say: "Put the cuffs on the bastards," and they say, "What the hell's this guy in our midst for, as a guest speaker, telling us some of our fellow businessmen are ripping us off. Geez, is he some kinda Commie or socialist?"

Socialism is a word businessmen never use in Canada. Socialism has never arrived in Canada, it's one word that has been not allowed. You can blame the Liberals for that more than anybody. Cause if they hadn't been able to steal socialist ideas from the CCF-NDP they never would've stayed in power for the last forty-fifty years. That's precisely the way they've been able to do it. By stealing all the socialist ideas and calling them Liberal ideas.

What do you think family allowance is, giving a woman money for having a baby – that, my friend, is socialism. What do you think veterans' allowance is, giving some old vet money for serving his country – that's socialism. What about rent control – that is socialism. Who's it practised by? The Progressive Conservative Party of the province of Ontario which is the government of Ontario and has been for god's sake ever since Adam was a little baby. Sure, *that* is socialism. What is old age pension? *That* is socialism. We got socialism all over the damned place only we don't like to admit it.

When anybody comes along sounding a little bit like a Ralph Nader, geez, the business boys get all tight over that one. That's when the old license on the wall to rob their fellow man starts to quiver. O geez, do they ever hate that!

So, the housing shortage in Canada's one of the wickedest,

rottenest things that was ever allowed to happen. And not one Canadian newspaper's ever had the balls to rise up and talk about it. And do stories on it. And get to the bottom of it. And discuss the real ripoff that exists in this country where, again, I repeat, we have more capital, more labor, more knowhow than anywhere in the world. Tell me we don't have the material to put up houses in this country, and tell me – if you can – that we don't have the space for houses. You don't have space for houses when you allow people to own land; you don't have the space to allow people to breathe air when you allow people to own the air they're going to breathe. And that's the little box we're in right now. So you can have all the Margaret Trudeaus, with jugs on their heads, walking around downtown Vancouver for the cause of pure water, you can have people running around shouting from the rooftops during International Womens Year with a badge saying "Why Not?" on their left tit – it don't mean nothing. It's all part of the golden age of bullshit. Which we're all living in, and wallowing in, and loving, and anyone who talks against it and really sees it for what it is, he's suspect, someone they oughta string up, and nail his wrists to a cross, and crucify cause the s.o.b. is spoiling the game. Well, I love spoiling the game. I think it's a scandal and I wonder how much longer we're gonna keep going with it. How long *will* we live with it? We'll live with it for a long time cause we don't have the guts to do anything about it. We don't have anyone concerned who could ever have the brains to put a government together in this country. So we'll start right with the people we got and that's the people we're stuck with. They're the ones got an exclusive for sure. They're gonna be in, year in and year out. We've never had a two-party system in the history of this country. We've had one outfit that's had an exclusive priority on the political brains of the country and the knowhow on how to be in the power business, which, when translated, means the government business. And that's the Liberals. Unless you think poor old Eldon Woolliams out of Calgary, or poor old Joe Clark is gonna be the answer. No way in the world. These other suckers know exactly how to stick it in and break it off. They'll cry "unfair!" The facts are, the Canadian people cannot buy houses. That is the fact. In the 1970s, in this golden age, Canadians starting out in life, marrying, supposedly putting a home together, raising a family, and being big-sucker consumers to keep the whole of the damned Chamber of Commerce and the Canadian Manufacturers Association in business forever, they cannot cut the mustard when it comes to buying a house. *That* has been one of the achievements of the people who dabble and fiddle around with land investments and real estate. And, it's all happened as a result of their divine right to do so under the government apparatus of this country at the federal, provincial and local levels. The people have been fooled.

There's no houses for people in this country. There's houses for money. And unless you got 100 grand, you're going to live in a shit house. ●

4
Horse Feathers & Horse Tales

Geez, we was sitting around the boarding house one night, just talking and gassing about horseracing. Winnie said she knew it was getting close to opening day. Boomer, my old pal from the Ford days, and Winnie, who's become a real close friend, and me has been going to the Greenwood opening day for about ten years now. Winnie says, "Fred, your legs is getting awful sweaty." It's always like that in the winter months before the bugle'd sound again for the opening of the season. Used to be the same old bullshit every year, opening day you know, you'd see some fellow, you never knew his name but you was always comfortable with him, you always talked with him either in the walking ring, or the betting ring or outside near the rail, or something. "Geez," they'd always say, "by geez, you've wintered well you know," and we all giggle a little and cackle. Everyone had a lot of anticipation, you know. It was a new season, new fresh bankrolls that were organized to get up to the front and do battle.

I mind one time, by geez, it was during the off season, it just seemed like spring was never going to come, you know what I mean. You almost felt you'd never switch on the radio and hear Gordon Sinclair, the old devil, say he'd seen a tit on his way up to Georgian Bay. He always used to do that you know, just to get 2,000 listeners calling him up to say what a dirty old man he was. Well, you've gotta get up pretty early in the morning to whip the likes of him, you know. He'd always say, "Good morning, ladies and gentlemen." He'd give you the date, and so on, the weather and then he'd say, "I seen a tit today." O geez, would he get an awful kick outa that but he'd ruffle everyone's feathers pretty good.

Off season, it's a good time to go over some of the old racing stories. I think a racing man's more honest in the off season when he's apt to crack about the odd caper he's pulled, you know what I mean. Once the season starts and the heat's on to get in the winner's circle, geez, most of them clam up, you know, you can't get nothing outa them.

There's nothing keeps a horseplayer more interested than a big payoff, you know. If he's ever gotta grievance, putting a couple of long shots together in a double, or running a ten dollar bill up on three or four races, like in a crap game where you just leave the dough there and you keep handling the dice cause they're hot, gets that old brain really clicking.

Racing's not like war where you can win a battle and lose the war; in racing it's the other way round. When you win a battle it kind of makes up for losing the whole damn war. Racing is a lot of fun when you're winning. At Vancouver we used to go out to the old Lansdowne on Lulu Island and we used to take the interurban or go on the track bus, or if we was real lucky maybe bum a ride or something to Marpole and hope that the old bridge would be open for the traffic. The track officials used to keep a beady eye open – they looked like a bunch of pirates with telescopes up on the roof of the stand at Vancouver – they'd have their lamps right on the Marpole bridge and when she was swung wide open to let the fish boats through and the cars couldn't get over it they knew a whole lotta customers wasn't going to get to the track as the traffic wasn't moving. So they'd hold the horses up, they'd have a red light flashing there; by geez, you had some of the longest post parades in the history of racing. The bastards would leave the paddock and about an hour later they'd finally get them inta the gate. I can remember the head of the mutuel wickets standing on an orange crate seeing an old Chinaman open his wallet, and after the moths all flew out of it the mutuel boss says, "Here it comes, he's coming with a sawbuck, hold everything." The guy come up and ask for his horse, as soon as he done that, geez, the bell went, the machines locked, and the horses were on their way. Poor bastard nearly dropped dead from shock with the noise of the whole thing.

The old bus to Lansdowne used to start out at the BC Electric headquarters. Geez, just getting on that bus to get out to the track for the first race was quite a production. I mind the time we were there with Morris, the old telephone man, used to handle all the bets on the telephone for the bookmakers, lived in a old rundown hotel right in the soft underbelly of Vancouver. Morris was on the bus, sitting in the back, and he had a lot of money to put down for certain parties. He couldn't understand why the bus wasn't taking off and there was a whole buncha fellows sitting there, all chatting away the way people do before a race. You can hear a pin drop after the day's over, but there we was all sitting there. Morris finally says, "Geez, Fred, what the hell's wrong? What's the matter with the driver, sitting up there reading the newspaper, not even looking at the *Form*, not even looking at the sheet, don't give a goddamn about anything."

I said, "I don't know what the trouble is. Why don't you go and ask him."

Geez, he goes up and says, "Hey, driver, when the hell are we going to get out of here?" and everyone looks up. I never thought to ask but Morris was a bit impatient, he used to be on a hot brick all the time. Driver says, "We aren't going until we get two more passengers." Morris says, "What!" Driver says, "Yeah. Each seat's a buck on this thing; we gotta get two more passengers and when she's a full load, it's my orders to let her rip." Morris pulls out two bucks and says, "Let's go now, you sonofabitch." And away we went.

Getting to the track is often half the fun. One time I was down in New York for the races at Belmont. Hotter'n a firecracker, musta been a hundred in the shade. There's nothing just like that city when the heat's on.

Well, there I was in Grand Central station, lost my bearings trying to figure out which train to take out to the racetrack on Long Island. I was down on the train platform, down under the ground, you know, and there is *two* trains marked with little cards in the windows, "Races". I was just getting on one of them when a black bird, in a trainman's uniform, comes trotting along and says, "Where you going, fellow?" I says, "I'm going out to Belmont at Elmont." Ain't that funny? Belmont track's at a little town in Long Island called Elmont. Try to keep *that* straight after a good day at the track when you been celebrating not wisely but too well. Anyways, the black guy says, "Well, you better hop on that train to your right . . . that's the one for Belmont." We hadda a couple minutes laugh, playing around with Belmont-Elmont . . . nice guy, friendly.

I started to climb aboard the train and he says, "Hold on there, fellow, that ain't the car you want." Well, holy doodle. It was the train he showed me, what's wrong with the car? He didn't say nothing just pointed to another car up ahead. We argued about for a couple a seconds, and then, the train starts to move. So, I didn't have no chance to change cars, just swung up aboard the car and waved goodby.

By geez, I sit down in the car and this is the first time it ever happened in my whole life. I challenge anybody to prove they wouldn't've acted the same. I sit down, and look around me, and there ain't a white man besides me in the car. Black guys, every one. Geez, I feel like lighting out for Canada but I'm on a moving train.

I remember it was 1950, the year Noor was a real big horse on the US tracks. Noor's running that day at Belmont, first time I seen him, and he's going against Hill Prince who was owned by Christopher Chenery, Penny Tweedy's father; the Mrs. Tweedy who owned Secretariat, same outfit, outa Virginia.

I knew Eddie Arcaro was gonna ride Hill Prince and old Johnny Longden, the Canadian, was coming from California to ride Noor. The race was the two-mile Jockey Club Gold Cup and everybody in racing was talking about it. One reason was that Arcaro had been having a hell of a time, hadn't ridden a winner in something like eighty-six races. That's a long dry spell for a jock the likes of Arcaro.

So I'm sitting in this railway car fulla blacks and I look at the guy I'm sitting beside. Great, big, black guy, had on a salmon-pink hat, a yellow shirt, and a big setta sand-colored jeans and white boots. Real dude, you know . . . lotsa horseplayers dress up real fancy, you know, like they think a certain shirt or a certain paira shoes bring them luck. This guy was reading his *Form* and counting hundred-dollar bills in his lap. I says to him, friendly like, I says, "Geez, Arcaro ain't been doing too good lately?" I admit, I was kinda sucking up to him, just trying to ease the tension. Geez, if looks could kill I wouldn't be here now telling you this story. He says, "Don't talk to me, you pinky bastard!"

I flew outa there. I was outa that gate faster'n Hill Prince . . . O yeah, Hill Prince win and made Noor and Longden look like monkeys. But that guy's "pinky bastard" kinda smartened me up. By geez, I thinks, something's got his dander up.

It's a funny thing, the way people go with racing. Old Morris, the telephone man who couldn't bear sitting on the bus while the driver was waiting for two more passengers, geez, we took him out to Exhibition Park one afternoon and bet the card, we touted him all afternoon wrong – *never* had a winner. Think they had seven races in them days. Then we took him down to Ladner, BC, near the American border, for the trotting races. Three races on the card, two heats each, so there was six chances. Geez, Morris tapped out on all six. Matter of fact, that's the night they got Captain King beat, he never lost a race in the Fraser Valley in the last ten years or something. Then we got in the car and drove down to Seattle, Washington, for the Sunday card at the Longacres track in Renton where they build the Boeing bombers. They had a ten-race card and Morris tapped out on all ten. Clean sweep.

Next morning we're all sitting round the lobby of the hotel there and Morris gets off the elevator, shuffles toward the front door, and one of the guys who works the starting gate says, "Hey Mo, where're you going?" Morris says, "Who me? I'm going to a psychiatrist."

I've never known a horseman to take a back seat at saying anything. I guess the last time the CBC ever done an in-depth broadcast, without realizing they was doing it, was when they covered the 1948 King's Plate down at the old Woodbine on the lake in Toronto. That was the year Jim Speers had Lord Fairmond with Longden riding him who was from Winnipeg. Jim Fair had a horse name of Last Mark who was the last foal of old McTab . . . I think, she was twenty-nine years when the foal come along, so of course Jim called him Last Mark. All his horses was called Mark . . . Mark This and Mark That, like a fleet of steamers. And the rumor went round the racetrack that Jim had hid this one behind the shit pile, just so's he could get an extra year on him, you understand. Now, of course a race like the King's Plate, or the Kentucky Derby, or whatever, is restricted to three-year-olds. That's the age the horse can be if he's going to run in the race; can't be younger and he sure as hell can't be older.

In them days, before the King's Plate, you couldn't race outside the country, so the only shot you had before the race was the Plate Trial. Well, Fair passed the trials up and worked his colt in front of the public one Saturday, just so's he'd get used to the noise of the crowds, and the bands playing, and so on. Now, remember, he hadn't run him before so everyone was saying, "What's Jim pulling off here? Don't even run his horse in the trials and now all he does is parade the colt and we're supposed to take him serious!" Geez, he come up favorite in the race, has an apprentice jockey on him, won it easy, and bust the track record. First time I ever seen old Jim Fair all dressed up in his life, was in the winner's circle, and the crowd was real happy. If anyone ever represented the little man it was old Jim Fair, the Cainsville dirt farmer. And he'd put one over on the big boys . . .

The CBC man come up to Jim and says, "Congratulations, Mr. Fair, on winning the King's Plate," and Jim was all expansive, higher than a kite, had a funny fedora on with a thirty-foot crown to her and he says, "Well, thank you very much, son." And then this guy, the CBC announcer says, "How old's your horse there?" Well, if Fair ever come close to shitting himself in his life it was that time. If ever a question was not wanted it was that one. Course the guy didn't know what he was asking, didn't know whether they was ten-year-olds or two-year-olds, cows or sheep. He didn't know what the hell the race was for. But that was probably the last in-depth question ever asked on the CBC . . . in 1948.

Old Jim Fair was pretty sharp, you know. One day a woman tackles him in the parking lot of the old Thorncliffe Park. She says, "Geez, you run five horses today, Mr. Fair, and you was all dressed up like Astor's horse, I thought you was going to really try. Looked to me like you had your cracking pants on." Old Jim says, "Well, that's too bad. You figured I was all dressed up cause I was getting ready to have my picture taken." She says, "That's right." He says, "Well, you made one awful mistake cause I had to go to a funeral this morning and I didn't have time to change."

He was right sharp. Kid comes up to him at Stamford one time . . . he had about twenty kids working for him . . . and the kid says to him, "Mr. Fair, we've only got two eggs left." Fair says, "Fry one for me and scramble the other for the rest of you."

Take old Butch Taylor, before he'd saddle Alias, you knew he was really on the job. Geez, you could tell he was up to something cause he took his clackers right outa his mouth and put them in a side pocket. By geez, if he won he'd be wondering where the hell they was . . . couple times he had to pick them up right off the grass. Another real give away used to be a trainer name of May Smith, one of the few women trainers you'd see around the track in Vancouver. Well, geez, if she had a real good "cross-your-heart" bra on, you could tell that'd be the day with her. Didn't matter nothing if she'd been to a beauty parlor, that was kinda like camouflage or a smokescreen. But, by geez, if she had the old up-lift on, with the old narbs pointing straight out at you, you knew that'd be the day, and by geez, them sonsofbitches'd come home like trained seals. She'd be right there in the winner's circle. Often's the time I can remember her with something that'd been down the track its last five starts, would've needed a sherriff's posse to find it, by geez, she'd be right there with the uplift. She never knew how someone could hop on and bet the sucker right down.

Yeah. Racing's full of characters but I guess none was as good as old Willie Morrissey in his day. You know, he was so confident of Bunty Lawless in the 1938 King's Plate, he told Charlie Ayres, who was the publicity man for the Woodbine, "Charlie, providing they're in the first four, I'll bet dollar for dollar with anyone who's got a horse in Canada." Geez, Charlie went around, got a few bets, a few thousand against Bunty Lawless, but Morrissey wasn't content with that, he thought that was chicken feed. Finally, he says, "I'll bet my hotel. Bunty Lawless against anyone and they gotta finish in the first four." He was a real high roller. Course Bunty Lawless win the plate that year, he was by Ladder who got burned up in a fire at Thorncliffe, out of a mare name of Mintwina that Morrissey got a hold of outa spite. Fellow took a horse of his outa a race, claimed it as was his right to do, and Morrissey took revenge on him, and drove over and claimed the guy's mare, Mintwina, right off him, and then immediately arranged to mate her. The fluke, of course, was that the progeny was Bunty Lawless, one of the best racehorses Canada ever seen. So good he win at the races, I mean at the Big Apple, he win down at Saratoga couple years running and believe me *that* takes some doing.

I remember years later old E.P. Taylor come up to Morrissey . . . and, of course. Taylor had a hell of a horse name of Windfields (named his farm after Windfields), and *he* was by Bunty Lawless . . . Taylor come up to Morrissey when the queen was at the new Woodbine. Taylor, of course, built the new Woodbine, proud as punch of the place, went up to Morrissey . . . Morrissey was a real rough diamond, sold newspapers on the corner, crap shooter, and you name it, you know what I mean . . . Taylor come up to him and says, "Bill, would you like to meet the queen?" Geez, Morrissey looks up at Taylor and says, "Naw, I don't want to meet the queen." Well, that sure got Taylor's silk shorts into a knot. He walked away saying, "That Bill Morrissey is just a goddamned guttersnipe."

You know, the best racing's in Toronto, no two ways about it.

That'll get a few of the old professional provincialites across the country up in arms. But no matter where you go, what country you're in, there's always a centre for racing . . . the best racing in the United States is in New York, the best in France is at Longchamps, in Paris, the best racing in England's at Ascot. Now, I'd say the best betting public, so far as betting dollar per capita as they like to say, no question about it – is Edmonton, Alberta, of all places. Geez, do they ever take the elastic off the roll out there; they bet like money's going out of style. I guess the best hospitality would be a dead heat with old Assiniboia Downs in Winnipeg with Jim Wright and maybe Connaught Park in Aylmer, Quebec, with the crazy old Gorman brothers. They're a sharp pair. Geez, the French call it *Parc Coconut*, ain't that a dilly?

When it comes to the hand of friendship, you gotta get up early in the morning to beat the Gormans, they're just terrific. The best food, the best grub at any track in Canada, is served in Vancouver. Remember when old Bob Ahearn, a racing man who's been all over the North American continent was talking to Joe Gorman one day. Colonel Ahearn as we used to call him, he used to tell all kinda lies like bout the time he stood on the buckboard with Matt Winn the first time the derby was ever run in Louisville – that's when Aristides win it. O, he was an awful fellow. He had a real good job at Arlington Park in Chicago as a publicist. Old Joe Gorman was kidding him along and says, "Well, when you worked in Toronto, didn't they give you a limousine, and a suite to live in, and a big posh desk, and a big-breasted secretary to answer every whim?" Ahearn says, "What? What are you talking about?" And Joe says, "Well, you just mentioned how when you're arriving in Chicago to start another meet they always meet you with a limousine. Geez, didn't the Jockey Club do that in Toronto?" Ahearn cracked right back, "Geez, the Jockey Club wouldn't meet you at the fucking bus station!"

You know, in the old days the racetrack operators used to say they was conducting the meet "for the improvement of the breed." That was supposed to be the idea behind it. Course, nowadays it's all supposed to be to help the various provincial and state treasuries. I'll tell you something; people say to me, "Fred, can you beat the races?" and of course there's an old saw that says "you can beat a race but you can't beat the races." Damon Runyan, who was about as knowledgeable as any about horseracing said, "All horseplayers die broke." But it's my feeling after my experiences down through the years that if the take-out or "grab" – the "bite" on the dollar – was down to about ten percent, I think a fellow with a good understanding of racing, what we'll call "good common-sense betting," and a good awareness of the whole situation, I think if the take-out was down to ten percent a fellow could make a darn good living. Trouble is, wherever you're playing now, you're up to sixteen, seventeen and a half, nineteen percent take-out, and they're just grabbing too much.

Most people can never figure that out but it's real simple: If you have a bunch of fellows over to your place and you told them that every time they played a hand of cards you was gonna grab a percentage out of the pot, well, it's pretty easy to see that if they had eight or nine cracks at it, and you grabbed sixteen, or seventeen, or nineteen percent of the pot at each crack, pretty soon there'd be no money left. Well, that's the trouble with the races. People always overlook the fact that every time they go up there and bet two bucks, someone's reaching in and taking, if not thirty-five cents, then about forty cents, before anything else happens. That's the real problem.

I really believe that, and I couldn't give a good goddamn if anybody says, "O, he's full of it; he don't know what he's talking about." I *do* know what I'm talking about. I'm telling you that if they wasn't so damned greedy nowadays and grabbing so much, a fellow who really works at it could go out and do real good. And, as far as that goes, I know of a few people that still is able to make it work but, otherwise, it's pretty much a mug's game. No two ways about it.

A lot of things change, you know. When I think about when I started out in the old days, there was no starting gate – you walked up to the start. O geez, did the horsemen ever get hot when it was suggested they had to break out of a starting gate. They used to say, real surly like, "There's no way I'm going into that Meccano contraption with my colt – I won't allow it." Horsemen got to be the most reactionary people in the world.

Course, most of them has always been opposed to testing. In my day, the big test used to be the saliva test. Well, you could beat *that* real easy. Then, of course, they come along with the urine test, and the way you got around that, when the fellow come down to your barn, many's the time your horse is tied up in some way and can't pass water, so we used to take the testing bottle and go in the corner of the stall, and take a leak into her and hand it back to him. Well, that was okay if you hadn't had no coffee during the afternoon, but if you had, the test would register positive cause the caffeine would light the whole sky up. You get the idea? Geez, couple guys in my days has been caught cause the colt they was running grabbed their windbreaker in the paddock, and maybe they spilled some coffee on their arm at breakfast. O yeah.

Back in them days, the *Racing Form* cost twenty-five cents and you asked for your horse by his name. It wasn't until after World War II that you come along and asked for a number when you was betting them. Geez, we used to have a laugh at the old Toronto tracks in the old days, there was a mare running round the Toronto circuit named Wanna Do It. I mind the time a woman come up to one of the sellers at the two-buck wicket, and she says, "Wanna Do It." And the guy behind the counter there, the guy with the tickets in front of him, says, "Well, not now lady, maybe later." O . . . did she ever get *her* bloomers in a knot. Them days is gone, though, nowadays you call them out by numbers, all kinda different.

I know a lotta things is changed, a lotta horses is running on hormones, and what they call "steroids." Butazolodin – that's even legal in some states, pain killers, you know what I mean. I mind old Angus MacPherson, a wonderful old Scotchman in Vancouver, he had a real good horse named Princes' Street, named after the main street of Edinburgh. Old Angus, geez, he was a trainer from the old school and one day they was razzing him pretty good there in the morning. He looked back at them and said, "I'll tell you one thing about Princes' Street: he's the fastest horse in Vancouver, and I'll tell you another thing about him: he's the only sonofabitch running on oats and hay in this city." By geez, you could hear a pin drop.

The boys looked right down at their shoes cause they knew old Angus was on the level.

Geez, could Princes' Street ever rattle on them turns. Other than Hi-Drive I don't think I ever saw a horse fly on a bend the way Princes' Street could. He was real quick through the lanes, but on them sharp turns he could accelerate, he could be in last hole and then in front before you could blink an eye. He just blasted wide open inta them turns.

There's an old saw, you know, that says "horseracing's the sport of kings." The reason for that, of course, is they say only kings can afford it . . . that's nothing new round the racetracks. I've seen some pretty good horses in my time. I already mentioned Willie Morrissey's Bunty Lawless, Bob Hall and Ernie Hammond's George Royal . . . he was supposed to be called Royal George but they got the name mixed up at the Jockey Club in New York. People who wanna wrap themselves up in the maple leaf, they could shoot their mouth off about the fact that if you're registering a horse for racing in Canada, a thoroughbred, you gotta write to New York for permission to name him. That oughta get a few old nationalistic shorts in a knot.

Cool Reception was a hell of a horse, beautiful chestnut, had blond hair on him, you don't often see that. He put the Kentucky Derby winner, Proud Clarion, away on the turn for home at Belmont, in the Belmont Stakes, and then was put to a real tough drive by Walter Blum. By geez, Willie Shoemaker on Damascus hove up on the outside and went by him, and they found out later that Cool Reception broke his leg coming to the wire. He was a real good Canadian horse. We've had others. I guess when you get down to the top horses in this country, there's only one man comes to mind for raising and racing them, and that's Eddie Taylor. He had Victoria Park, a real good horse, third in the derby in his year and second in the Preakness; Taylor raised Cool Reception but sold him; he raised Nijinsky but sold him to Charlie Englehard. Taylor, of course, raised and raced Northern Dancer who won the Kentucky Derby *and* the Preakness in 1964 and got a third at Belmont; geez, at his yearling sale, Taylor had Northern Dancer up for sale at $25,000 which woulda been the bargain of the century for anyone smart enough to see what was going to happen when that colt started burning up the track.

Taylor tells the story about a Belmont Breakfast, a morning get-together at the track for owners, trainers, jockeys and the working press. This is a couple days before the Belmont. A reporter asks the trainer of Quadrangle, another horse entered in the stakes, "Can Quadrangle be rated?" Now, "rating" is track slang for taking the horse in hand and letting him have his head when you, the jockey, wants him to go. Kinda like putting a car from low gear inta high gear. Quadrangle's trainer says, "Yes, Quadrangle *can* be rated." Now, Taylor thinks to himself, "That's an interesting piece of news," cause just the week before, Taylor's jockey, Bill Hartack who's going to ride Northern Dancer in the Belmont, had been aboard Quadrangle in the Metropolitain Mile and reported that Quadrangle could *not* be rated. So, naturally, Taylor figures this is important news for him and Northern Dancer, and looks around the breakfast tables to see if Horatio Luro, Northern Dancer's trainer, had heard the same piece of news. He catches Luro's eye and they exchange signals and Taylor figures, "It's safe – Luro heard, too." You see, a trainer has to worry about his own horse, but if he's a *good* trainer, he's also concerned about the competition. So Taylor figures his trainer heard the news about Quadrangle and will instruct Hartack to take the appropriate moves in the stakes in a couple days.

Well damn, as Taylor now tells the yarn, Luro did *not* hear the news and went into the Belmont Stakes instructing Hartack to ride Northern Dancer as if Quadrangle could not be rated. Well, that little bit of confusion cost Taylor the Triple Crown, which must've hurt, and a few thousand bucks he could well afford to drop. Northern Dancer come a miserable third behind Quadrangle and Roman Brother. That was the end of Northern Dancer's hope for the Triple Crown. But he was still a hell of a horse.

In California, once, Louis B. Mayer tried to buy Man o'War off Samuel Riddle for a million bucks. When he turned Mayer down, Riddle said, "Mr. Mayer, there are thousands of people in the United States with a million dollars. But there's only one Man o'War; I've got him and I'm going to keep him. Save your million dollars." Mayer didn't get that colt but he spent other millions on his stable. He often had to accept the humility of being booed when his horses would finish a race one-two-three. It used to be a thing for people to boo *any* kinda successful or rich owner. It's a kinda unpleasant thing, it's a yahoo thing, almost as if people think the owner himself is there in his shorts running around the track, so they're saying, "Who are you, you rich sonofabitch, get out of my way." Nasty thing. I've never liked it. I think when a horse is out there, he's doing the best he can and it don't matter to me who owns him.

A funny thing. Taylor brought Northern Dancer back to Toronto for what turned out to be his last race at the Woodbine in the Queen's Plate in 1964. Luro hada great big black fellow acting as a groom. The big guy leads Northern Dancer into the walking ring; the place is packed, geez, people were ten-fifteen deep all around the walking ring, *everyone* wanted to see the horse from Canada that'd gone to Churchill Downs and won the derby. Except for Paul Henderson scoring three goals against the Russians in the first Team Canada effort against Russia, there probably was never any greater moment in Canadian sports than on that first Saturday in May, in 1964, when Northern Dancer beat Hill Rise by a neck in that derby. I can still see him bursting outa the pack at the head of the lane, just going hellbent for leather, and, by geez, Hartack riding like Wild Bill Cody, and everybody saying, "O dear god, let the little colt hang on!" And remember, Willie Shoemaker was up on Hill Rise, and justa few weeks before Shoemaker had hurt every fan of Northern Dancer's by saying he didn't want to ride the Canadian colt, but would take his chances on Hill Rise. Geez, Willie brings Hill Rise right up alongside Hartack on Northern Dancer but Bill gives the colt a lick of the stick and he spurts out in front again. I think . . . I honestly think they could've gone round that track another time and Northern Dancer would still've beat Hill Rise. As old Brian Fielding, the caller, said, "He held him even, got up to a neck but, by geez, he held him even."

When Northern Dancer come into the walking ring at Woodbine, I'll never forget it as long as I live. He stood up on his hind legs, you don't often see a racehorse do that, very rare, like a bear standing there begging for a treat. His forelegs was tucked up like a boxer's arms. Geez, the wind blew through his mane, you could hear a hush spread through that crowd. All of a sudden, everyone started clapping, kinda polite, a lotta restraint like they knew that heavy applause would frighten the horse. From that day on I've never heard E.P. Taylor booed on a Canadian racetrack. Even for the old two-buck plunger, Taylor ended up being the guy who went down and set the Americans right on their arse. The fact that he had a lotta money, and a lotta power, and a lotta privilege, it was still good enough for the working fellow to know that there's all kinds of men who spent fortunes trying to win the derby and never come close. Taylor was – and still is – kinda looked upto on tracks right across this country.

I remember another "last appearance" of Northern Dancer. He was training for the Travers at Saratoga, and they said he ruptured a tendon, but I think he bowed a tendon. They brought him out for one more time around the track, a walk-around. Geez, I tell you, I was standing there with my pal Boomer, and we looked around, and there was a couple big Hoosiers, truck drivers, a pair of real rough stones, standing behind us, and, by geez, just as Northern Dancer goes walking by on his farewell trip, I looked at them two birds and there was tears coming down their cheeks. It's not going to be too often the likes of them are going to get all caught up like that. So, you see, Taylor's kinda made magic in racing. He is the man who's put it on the map, and he's the one fellow I know of who's had the vision to see the whole thing work out. There's an awful lot of people who oughta get down on their prayer handles and thank Allah or Muhammad for the likes of E. P. Taylor.

By geez, if you've stuck with me this far it'll come as no shock that I'm kinda fonda horseracing. I like lottsa sports but racing's Number One for sure. But I gotta make one thing awful clear: Northern Dancer, in this here book, is called Northern Dancer – never The Dancer. O geez, I'd never ever think of calling him just The Dancer. That's cause way back in 1953 when Alfred Vanderbilt raced Northern Dancer's granddaddy on his dam's side, Native Dancer was the first North American TV horse. He was a light gray, and on black-and-white TV in them days, you could always

see him. He was always running a long way outa it, and then he'd
come with a Hollywood stretch run, and get up there and he done
it every time he run. Every time except for one time in the 1953
derby when old Hank Moreno beat him on Dark Star. Native
Dancer was called The Dancer, that was *his* nickname. It just
turned my stomach when Northern Dancer come along in 1964
and the whole of Toronto's racing press started calling him The
Dancer.

A whole lotta other people all over North America done the
same dang thing when Secretariat was big in 1973; they called him
Big Red. The nickname Big Red belongs to Man o'War – he was
Big Red. Man o'War was Big Red, and I've always thought, geez,
ain't they gotta little more imagination than that? After all, in
racing you could no more send the name Northern Dancer in now
for a horse; you'd be disqualified on two counts. First, you have to
wait fifteen years to repeat a name. Second, there's some names
that's famous that they don't allow to be repeated. You can't have a
Man o'War. I remember in harness racing, Brand X, I call it, geez,
some fellow named a trotter or a pacer Man o'War. I don't think
he was any good either. I don't think he could trot worth a damn,
but I was always upset when they fooled around with the names
and took the nicknames of great horses from the past.

Vanderbilt, Native Dancer's owner, was always real sharp at
naming horses. Native Dancer's sire, his daddy was Polynesian and
his momma, his dam was Geisha Girl, so Vanderbilt looked at them
two names and came up with Native Dancer. Gotta be one of the
best-named horses in a long time, a Polynesian geisha girl.

I can think of a lotta funny things that's happened with names of
horses and naming horses. There's an old saying, you know, that
once you put someone's name on a horse, he'll be no good. I think
they just destroyed one named Glennie after the hockeyplayer.
Broke down as a four-year old maiden, never would win, all sortsa
them like that.

I guess the American Triple Crown is racing's most important
piece of jewelry. Actually, there ain't no single medal nor cup nor
nothing signifying the winner of the Triple Crown, but you can
wager your best shirt there ain't a horseplayer nowhere in North

America that don't know the horse that wins the Triple Crown. (I guess a British horseplayer might argue that England's Triple Crown was just as important, but I'm writing this here for Canadian readers and the American Triple Crown is tops.) Just to give you an idea, in the long and honorable history of the Triple Crown, only nine horses – each of them only three years old when they win – has won all three in any one year. The three races that make up the triple Crown are the Kentucky Derby at Churchill Downs, Kentucky; the Preakness Stakes at Pimlico, Maryland; and the Belmont Stakes at Belmont Park, New York.

A million years ago – or so it seems to horseplayers – a Montreal owner named Commodore J.K.L. Ross had a terrific colt name of Sir Barton. And he win the first Triple Crown – yeah – a Canadian-owned horse – in 1919. Now, the three races that make up the Triple Crown had been in business for a long time before that. But, the job of putting together three firsts at three of the continent's really prestige-y meets had never been done before Sir Barton done it in 1919.

I guess that was probably the first time the ordinary man-at-the-track in the US of A ever took notice that there was a country up there to the north. Surer'n hell it was the first time a lot of horseplayers ever thought about Canada being a power on the dirt or grass oval. Geez, imagine how we'd feel if the Ruskis wooshed in and won the Stanley Cup away from *Les Canadiens*. Down through the years only eight other horses ever met the mark set by Sir Barton. Course, like I said before that's what made it so special when Northern Dancer comes within a whisker of doing it again in 1964.

Austin Taylor of Vancouver once had a real good colt named Indian Broom. Indian Broom was American bred – and so was Ross's Sir Barton – and in 1936 finished third in the derby. So along comes Eddie Taylor and he gets a third in 1960 with his Victoria Park in the derby, and then he gets a second in the Preakness with Victoria Park. And he comes right back in 1964 to win the derby with Northern Dancer and the Preakness, too. Taylor was denied his Triple Crown when there was all that confusion over whether Quadrangle could be rated, but I already told you about that. Course, it was Northern Dancer's son, Nijinsky, who won the English Triple Crown of the Two Thousand Guineas, the English Derby, and the St. Leger in 1970. He was probably the greatest Canadian-bred horse of all time. Taylor didn't own Nijinsky – he'd sold him for $84,000 to Charlie Englehard.

Old Connie Smythe's a pretty sharp old horseman, too, you know. He was famous for all kinda things, most I guess for being the "father" of the Maple Leaf hockey club, being the real instigator behind the putting up of the Maple Leaf Gardens. You gotta get up pretty early in the morning to whip Conn Smythe when it comes to working your arse off for some kinda charitable cause. You can ask anyone connected with the crippled children, or the deaf. . .O geez, Conn Smythe is an awful tough act to follow.

He's had a terrific lotta success at racing. Course not many people know it, but once he had a horse name of Rare Jewell, and as he says himself, "in them days I didn't know nothing about racing and that's why I bet on the mare." Rare Jewell was in the Coronation Stakes for two-year-olds, geez, the horse paid $214 for a two-buck ticket.

Smythe's got a wonderful sense of humor. He minds the time he was working for his dad down at the old Woodbine. In them days there was no betting windows, or parimutuels, or tote boards; the bookies stood round in the crowd, quoting odds and taking bets. One of the *grandes dames* of Canadian racing at the time was a woman name of Mrs. Stephens. The first day he went to work young Smythe heard the bookmakers calling out, "Scratch Mrs. Stephens's Monkey!" and he wondered just what kinda weird fleshpot he was going to work in. Old Conn still chuckles when he tells that one on himself.

Smythe says he has lived his whole life guided by the philosophy that "the boss's footsteps makes the best fertilizer." And he says, "Show me a jock who is doing real good with fast horses, fast cars, and fast women and I'll show you the same kid ending up on the junk pile with slow horses, slow cars, and something worse than both of them together – slow women."

It was old Chattahoochee Smith said it was "love, care, and kindness" that gets to a horse. I also mentioned how reactionary most horsemen is. One of the nicest things that ever happened around a racetrack happened cause of an economic situation. Lotta women working at the track nowadays that you never seen before, and that's cause an awful lotta fellows figure that working around horses is beneath them. That happened with the black fellows, you know. In the old days a black guy could always get work round the track; in fact, one of the best jockeys of all time was a black man, Isaac Murphy. So a lot of women's moved in now, working as hot-walkers, grooms, and exercise gals. Most horsemen who hire them will tell you one thing about them: They got that love, they got that ability to care, they got that kindness and patience, and they're a lot better most of the time around horses than men is. Kinda interesting.

And, now that I'm on the subject of women at the track, I might as well say I ain't going to get into a stupid argument about whether women jockeys is as good as men jockeys. The answer to that was given by Robin Smith, the best female "jockette," – geez, I *hate* that word – in the United States. She herself says that when it comes to the actual physical exertion, there's no way she's got the strength at her command that an Angel Cordero has when it comes to two horses hooking head to head and driving right for the wire with all the leather being used that god ever told the other fellow about. When it comes to love, care, and kindness, on the racetrack women seem to have the patience to work longer, they're more conscientious, to put the time in, to really care. It ain't a job for them, it's love. There's a funny thing, about women and horses, a lot of fellows who've raised daughters will tell you there's a funny kinda period in the lives of young girls when they have a kinda love affair with a horse. They'll comb it, and ride it, and look after it, and brush it, and feed it, standing bug-eyed looking at it, and stroke it, and fondle it. That's a funny thing that happens to a lotta young girls. I'm not saying that women is the be-all and end-all, that they got all the answers. I'm just saying that around the racetrack, if you was to go up to any trainer that employs women, and I'm thinking of Johnny Campo in New York and Arthur Warner in Toronto, they'll say, "Why do you think I only have women working in my barns? Cause when I tell them to do something, I know they're going to do it right, and I know it's going to be right cause they care."

There's another phenomenon in racing, a groundswell for a lotta new things – Sunday racing, off-track betting. Sooner or later we're going to get over the idea that if you go out to the track, and bet at the track through the parimutuel machine, that's a legal thing to do, and you're within your rights to do it. But, if you bet away from the track, you're breaking the law. It seems to me a funny thing that you can phone up your broker and buy a patch of grass for buffalo to graze on, and that's perfectly in order. But you can't call up someone and make a bet on a horse. That's still illegal. In Ontari-ari-ario, about five years ago, there was quite a parcel of off-track betting shops opened. Called OTB.

Now pay attention. Canadian Gypsum is fined $1,000 for polluting in Weston, outside of Toronto, making a smell like you'd think a quarter million people who'd been eating beans had gathered, just wicked, the air's so blue. Fined $1,000 and not a first offense either. Eaton's, Canada's largest finance company, doing $25 million worth of business a week, fined $1,500 for misleading advertising. And a poor s.o.b. of a bookmaker, or off-track messenger man in Cayuga, Ontario, fined $175,000 by the Ontario government!

If that don't show priorities I don't know what does. One hundred and seventy-five thousand dollars! A thousand for polluting, fifteen hundred for misleading advertising, and a poor bookmaker, one hundred and seventy-five thousand dollars! *There's* the priorities in Ontari-ari-ario. So what's happened to OTB? It's still something that has to be attended to by the federal government. Until the federal government amends the federal Criminal Code to allow the province to go into the OTB business you'll never have it . . . they come close to it once with John Turner, they even had it going and then parliament dissolved.

The whole thing's a joke anyways. If you talk to any bookmaker he'll tell you that only about ten to fifteen percent of his action is on horses, the rest is all on football, hockey, basketball, baseball. The whole thing's ridiculous. You can go into a betting shop in Australia, France, Great Britain . . . geez, there's no problem whatsoever. You just tell them what you want to do and it's all legitimate. Here – in Canada – you're a criminal. The whole thing's ridiculous cause it gives the real criminal boys a shot at getting their hands on some real money to finance some things that to them is really important, and as far as the rest of us goes that is really scarey.

You know, the English are the only people who'll take a word like derby and turn it into something like darby. It's like the old regimental sergeant-major, you know, he's got the boys all lined up there, the first day, all in their old civvie suits, not looking too sharp. By geez, he comes along and starts calling off the roll, comes to a fellow, and he says, "Inglis, step forward." Nothing happens, nobody steps forward. Well, the old soldier's kinda ruffled by this and he says, "Alright, if you blokes don't know your own names I'll spell them out for you," and he spells out I-N-G-L-I-S and a meek looking little guy steps out of the first row and marches up to the sergeant. Sergeant says, "What's your name, soldier?" Guy says, "Ingles, sir." "What the hell are you talking about?" the sergeant bellows. "If your name was Ingles it would be spelled different; your name is spelled I-N-G-L-I-S and it's pronounced Inglis and don't you forget it."

Way back in Year One, when thoroughbred racing was first jammed down the throat of the Church of England from the pulpit by the king of them days, a couple of birds by the name of Bunberry and Derby met, tossed a coin, and decided on calling a race after the winner and, by geez, Bunberry lost out to Derby. If this hadn't gone the way it done, we would've had the Kentucky Bunberry, the Canadian Bunberry in Edmonton, the Bunberry Stakes at Epsom, and you name them. There's been a lot of Lord Derbys down through the ages. The present Lord Derby wrote a foreward to an awful joke of a book and I got the following story from it, only decent thing about the book.

The lord minds the time when he was asked to show his father's famous horse, Hyperion, at a real slick horse show. It was a real hot summer's evening. They brought out Hyperion, one of the great horses of all times, one of the horses that makes you believe that all modern-day thoroughbreds go right straight back to the Darley

Arabian, the Byerley Turk, Godolphin Barb, and such. They say in them days, when Hyperion raced in England, that there was *no* horse that ever looked better'n him. No man's eyes had ever been laid on a horse that was better'n Hyperion. He looked like the gods had finally got together and said, "for all them people interested in thoroughbred racing, why don't we just design something that's so perfect that no one can ever see a flaw in it?" That was Hyperion – except for one thing: he was tiny. O geez, people liked the little colt, but not many had much faith in him as a racer. Course, that's only natural. Horse trainers is funny, they like great big sonsofguns. My experience has been that the bigger they are the harder they fall, the easier it is for them to break down. Horses is awful fragile. Horses is like marriages and love affairs – fragile as all get out. You never know where the crack is, where the stress is, or the strengths. Hyperion – he was a Triple Crown winner in England – Hyperion was something else. He was something that every Cockney workman just used to boast about if he ever laid his eyes on the horse.

So, here was Lord Derby and he had his father's horse, Hyperion, now an old stallion retired at the age of twenty-nine. "Stallion's" a word that's used wrong all the time now in newspapers; I don't think there's hardly a sports editor knows the real meaning. If you're a stallion, that means you've dropped your stick, and you've serviced a mare, and you've done the job. That's when you're a stallion, that's the only way you *can* be a stallion. Most of the racing writers in this country call anything with balls on it a stallion. But until you've done the job, you are *not* a stallion. Well, Hyperion was a stallion, one of the best of this century. He sired Hydroplane II who was Citation's mother, the winner of the Triple Crown in 1948 in America. I could go on and on till the cows come home about what he done in his time standing in the breeding shed.

Anyways, here he was at the age of twenty nine, a real old man, but just as beautiful as ever. By geez, they brought him out in the show ring to show the horse lovers what the old champion looked like. Hyperion come into the ring, let out an enormous sigh and lies down, right in the show ring. And gol dang, if he ain't got an enormous erection, a horse-sized hard on. There's the champion, as beautiful as he had been at the peak of his career, standing there proud like, with just a huge erection. Just as thousands was looking on, the guy running the lights plunged the joint into darkness and the poor old fellow was led out of the ring. ●

5
O, Valiant Heart,
Abide with Me

By geez, one of the fellows at the Orchard Park Tavern got inta an argument talking about the German general, Kurt Meyer, the fellow who was tried, and, I think, served time in Canada after the war. I think he was our only war criminal; in fact, old Clarence Campbell of the NHL was one of the birds on the Nuremberg trial deal there. That's a long time ago, a lotta water's gone under the bridge since them days. Geez, when Kurt Meyer got out, he went round one of the Canadian forces bases in Germany trying to sell them beer or something. I glory in our fellows' spunk – they threw him right out.

Remember he was the fellow who . . . I think his prisoners was put in shackles . . . then there was a big deal over him shooting some Canadians. We was sitting one night talking about it, and arguing about it, and, gosh, one fellow says he still wakes up, still has dreams, still remembers just how cold it was, how still it was, and how it all felt when he and some buddies was on patrol, and a buncha Germans give themselves up.

He says, "It's a funny thing what war will do to people. Sure, it may bring good out in some men, but it brings out some kind of beast in others." It's like on VE Day another fellow, I was working with one time, he said he seen the chief petty officer of his ship floating face down with a sorta bubble of air right through the back of his uniform, you could see his collar, his navy collar there. There was a knife right between his shoulder blades. Another time, I remember working in a warehouse and the fellow beside me says, "By geez, we made short work of the sonofabitch who was the CPO on our ship. Threw the bastard right off the stern . . . just went and got him out of his bunk and that was the end of him."

I remember an old pal of mine, out on the coast, was telling me about a . . . what a wonderful story it was too . . . he was telling me about how he was on guard duty, guarding some lorries in Italy, O, fifty-sixty miles behind the lines, he figured. Maybe I'm exaggerating, maybe it was only twenty-thirty. He used to go on duty, and fire a shot inta the air, and that'd keep the local Italians from stealing gasoline and tires off the vehicles that was parked there. It was about the only thing the Italian civilians at the time could do, wasn't no work, they had to hustle for a buck.

One night, outa the darkness, come a German with his hands up, speaking perfect English, said he was trying to surrender. This guy says, "I was on duty, I was guarding a good-sized parking lot of lorries, had a few buddies with me, British fellas, this was in the British Army. We took the guy aside and give him a cocoa, got him warm, everyone sat around and chewed the fat, we talked a little about the war. Then we figured . . . holy doodle . . . we've broke just about every regulation in the book. So, we sent him packing down the road . . . figured there's just no way we're gonna take him as a prisoner.

That morning the sergeant came through on his motorcycle, stopped and shouted out – 'Anything to report?' We said, Nothing to report, and the sergeant drove on. Tried to sell that story to the CBC Pacific region . . . wrote it all out as a play, sent the story in, and the fellow in charge of buying plays said that could never happen in the British army. Geez, did we ever get a laugh out of that!"

Another fellow I talked to, he was really impressed with what they called the German war machine. Geez, you could talk by the hour, to them fellows who've really studied it. They get a kick outa it. They could whip you with facts and figures anytime.

This one guy was saying one day there was a little boy running after a German truck pulling outa an Italian town there, and one of the fellows sitting on the tailgate of the truck just shot the kid right in the head. He says, "You know, when you see that, then you wonder just what the hell is going on, what are you dealing with."

Yet, you'll read stories of where a guy's puttering around all alone, he feels there's someone round, he turns round, and I know one guy, the god's honest truth, he's still living, still going, still on parade with the 19th Batallion. Says he's here cause some German had dead aim on him at about forty feet – point blank range – all he done, the German, was he just put his rifle up and walked away. "Now," he says, "I can still see the guy sitting there, crouching at the ready, aim, fire, done nothing, just stand up and walked away."

All sortsa stories about fellows in the Royal Flying Corps with no ammunition left, and once in awhile some German pilot's fella come along armed to the teeth, see they had nothing left, do a few loop the loops, rush by, scare the shit out of him, then fly away. Get your bullets, fellow, then we'll take you on. Course, that's when it's real romantic.

I remember old Freddie Busch, real nice fellow, he was another one of them Germans who never fought no British or no Americans or no Canadians or nothing, just fought the Russians. Sold vacuum cleaners or something when he was here in Canada, but he said he was leading the life of Riley in Paris when he got orders to go on a week's leave. Well, he didn't wanna do that, he'd met a girl there in Paris and he didn't even wanna go home. Anyways he's shifted to the Russian front and he said he soon found out what he was up against. He said he come across a buncha Russian soldiers, frozen to death with raw grain in their hands. When he got back to base that night he told his mates, "These people is fighting us and all they got going for them is raw grain!" He was told to just shut up, make no comment on anything, and he'll get on real good. He says, "What the hell does that mean?" He was told, "There's a lotta funny fellows turning up here. It's best just not to say anything to anybody. If you don't have the will to win, all of a sudden you just leave here, no one knows where ya go. It's best not to say nothing." He says, kinda desperate, "I'm not kidding you, they had raw grain in their hands . . . come across a whole pile of them. How the hell are we gonna beat someone like that?" Another fellow, an officer, he'd been there a couple of years, he says, "I agree with you; we're not gonna, but don't let on to them. All you gotta do is try and keep yourself as best as you can." Makes you wonder, don't it, when you read that book on all the Stalingrad letters. Did you ever see that? . . . all the letters they found that the Germans never did mail. The Germans *never* delivered them, figured it was best not to. Hitler thought it was defeatist. When Stalingrad fell he said he'd never appoint another field marshall in the German army and he never did, either.

You know, back in them days when the big war was on, Canada was pretty good. Speaking of the old cenotaph deals, I remember the time we hadda pretty darn good shindig at the Royal York Hotel one year in Toronto. Geez, there was a big turnout, real surprising, for no reason at all. Almost kinda like everyone gets the message, sorta like he has a premonition, better go down and see old so-and-so, see if old Teddy's lost any weight, or whatever. A lotta fellas I hadn't seen in a long time, we had a hell of a good time. Boys O boys, did we ever get inta the sauce pretty good. Wasn't like some of the shindigs, right after the war, when you took the furniture in the lobby and actually built positions, and then manned them on into the night. O, there was quite a bit of that in the old days. I could name you quite a few people who got absolutely corned out of their minds. Geez, sitting there yelling, "Ready, aim, fire!" O, holy blue geez.

Finally this night, it was time to form up outside the hotel, right in fronta the old Union Station there. I guess it was about 11:15 at night, quite cold as it often is. After about five minutes or so the old sergeant major come out and called the roll. No one laughed, or giggled, or nothing, we all acted like it was back in the old days. Geez, the sergeant takes it real serious, had a face on him like a torn-over shoe. Then we'd move to the right, and freeze, and with just the one drum. The damn thing sounded like it had a real wet head on it. Sounded like an old Eaton's suitbox being whacked by a big Chinese wooden spoon.

Anyways, we went on down to Bay Street and headed on up to the cenotaph right at the old City Hall there. Quite a march for some of the guys. Anyways, there was no talking as we approached the cenotaph at the City Hall, we was all ready for any society by that time. That's when you go through that funny kinda . . . that funny kinda . . . I guess it's sorta like intoxication, you kinda see yourself, and at the same time, though, you almost feel as though you're moving through molasses. You're laughing and you shouldn't be laughing, and yet you can kinda see in your mind's eye, you sorta photograph your movements, and you say, "Geez, do I look as drunk as I feel, can them people see me?" Anyways, you still got your bearings.

As usual we're too early, everyone jumping the gun. The old sergeant was looking at his watch at ten o'clock, at one time there, to shout the fall-in. We told him to forget it. Boys, did we ever come up with one horrible discovery after we got there and was standing in line – we forgot the wreath. Well, the last time I seen her, she was sitting in her box on the piano. So I told the sergeant major, I says, "Try right there on the piano in the room where we was having the singsong." Boys, he wasn't too happy about that at all. O geez, then he starts talking about who was in charge of the damn thing, ya know what I mean? But a real nice policeman come forward and he says, "Listen fellows, I'll shoot you back down there before you can say Jack Robinson in the car and you can get it." So I volunteered, cause no one else seemed to know anything about it, and within minutes, there I was going back through the Royal York, up the stairs, into the lobby and geez, where the hell we'd been. The way I was standing there, not too good a stance, I attracted a plainclothes man who came over to see what was going on. I told him we was having our annual veterans' dinner and march up to the cenotaph . . . told him we'd forgot the wreath. By geez, in no time at all I was in an elevator going up to the floor and there was this huge room still smelling of smoke, all the lights on, no one in it and the wreath sitting right there on the piano. I gotta real kick outa that.

I tell you, if ever I was happy to see a wreath, it was on that occasion. I guess it's cause you always build yourself up, you always figure some rotten so-and-so's gonna swipe something, and then when they don't do it, you're relieved, you sorta get yourself all prepared, you put yourself through something. Anyways, I thanked the house detective and hurried on down to the lobby and got back out. The policeman put his foot on the gas, geez, he even had the siren going. It was a lotta fun. We roared right back up Bay Street, it was about three minutes to midnight. We had some idea we hadda get there right in the nick of time.

Geez, it felt cold and damp and it was just starting to drizzle. November 11 weather. All of a sudden, there we was, back to square one, the whole outfit drew up in pretty good order, three sides of a square formation, each front rank about twenty feet or so from the base of the monument. The old City Hall clock struck the first bell of midnight and, by geez, the sergeant major had a man ready to handle the wreath, so I fell back inta my spot, and from then on everything just went like clockwork. Boys, I'll tell you, if ever anyone sobered up quick that night, it was the sergeant major and Freddy Dobbs. If anything straightened out our outfit that night, too, it was the boys standing there, waiting for the wreath, and finally the old "Last Post." It was one of them nights when the atmosphere was just alive, you get the sound of anything, you can even hear a cat's heart beating. When that bugle started, it was like the only bugle that was ever gonna blow. All them crosses at Vimy, they come back to me, all them other times at the cenotaph, they all come back to me, and the further back I went, the more fellows that was standing there, better looking too, they was, standing there.

Well, that's one of the things about all them dinners, there's really fewer men each year, the turnout might vary a bit, but by the time the old roll is called she's getting down. Tell you one thing, when they mark you absent, that's it. That's one thing about this old life that's for sure – death and taxes. And there's another thing you can put down too – you're dead one helluva long time. Not too long after midnight, then, we was all in a darn good column though, swinging down back Bay Street to the Royal York, got back at the old piano and some more white lightning. Bay Street and the old City Hall in Toronto has always had, O, I think a special kinda meaning to me, not cause it's the financial district, not that, and not cause it's the street with all the banks on it, but because well, I think I've seen so many things happen there.

In 1939, the year the king and queen come to Canada, I can remember seeing the Royal Marines Plymouth Division Band, they used to call it Rickets's Band. Old Harry Rickets was the bandmaster and he used to write all his marches under the pen name of Kenneth Alford. I guess anyone who knows their marches knows that Alford's . . . they call him Britain's Sousa . . . he's the guy who wrote "Colonel Bogey" and a whole pile of other marches. I can remember, just as I'm sitting here now, Rickets's band was playing at the CNE that year, and, O geez, was Rickets ever hot as hell at the CNE. You know, people used to get mad at the CNE director, even in them days. They wanted the band to play "Colonel Bogey" at every concert and Rickets was just sick, sore, and tired of the boys doing it at every concert. They probably had the best band outa Britain, the Royal Marines Plymouth Division Band, Rickets's Band, and here's the CNE director telling him to play "Colonel Bogey" at every concert. O geez, did that hot. He was a great bandsman you know.

They hadda get back home, of course. Germans crossed the Polish Corridor on September 1 . . . I think Britain declared war September 3 and by the time Mackenzie King got his parliament all together, with the members coming on the trains from one enda the country to the other, we got into it on September 10. Just towards the enda the CNE, in late August there, the band hadda go home and they hadda concert on the City Hall steps before leaving and they played the "Vanished Army," a march that he wrote for the fellows that didn't come back from the first war. Geez, you could hear a pin drop. The people was backed up right from the City Hall steps right across the other side where the old Bowles lunch was, right across the street . . . no traffic moving, or nothing, and then the band marched down Bay Street to the railway station. Geez, many just kinda stood there, but a lot marched with them just to keep hearing them. They played the entire way. I remember just standing there, and you could hear them even when they got down to Front Street you could still hear them, and I thought, by geez, once again Great Britain's been caught with her drawers down, but you gotta give the bastards credit.

You know, it was a funny thing, I could sorta sense everyone was gonna do the same thing all over again. Just as I could hear the last of that band going around the corner down by the station, I thought, "We'll be along. It'll take us a little while, but we'll get there, we'll be there." Geez, I found myself with the quickest step I'd had in about five months, going up Bay Street, didn't even know where the hell I was going. All of a sudden I had to admit I felt good.

The other day a fellow says to me when we were talking, he says, "Fred, you gotta admit that this country Canada's got the worst goddamn death wish god ever told the other fellow about. What is it, do you suppose?" Geez, when the CBC talks about Canadians in World War II, they go and do documentaries on Dieppe. What's it all about? Why do we have this funny thing about us? How is it we don't think enough of ourselves? Are we all brainwashed? Who's fault is it?

Maybe you can start with the lousy provincial education systems we got right clear across this country. Way back in the Year One, when the divine right to an education was considered bigger than sliced bread, somebody somewheres hadda come up with some kinda course of studies. I guess nowadays they call it the curriculum. Way, way back there, O geez, back in them days schools used to be interested in reading, writing and arithmetic . . . remember that, the three Rs they used to call it. But nowadays, with democracy in action, you got the right to use your undeveloped brains . . . this don't make no damn sense at all, well that's appropriate, it's education.

I was told the whole point to education was to teach you how to think, funny how that point's been missed somewheres along the way. No denying the kids has learned a lot nowadays, so much so that their old man and their old lady can't help them the way ours used to in the old days. Them days . . . well, they used to call them the good old days but I ain't gonna let things get that thick. I do think, maybe, we kinda had some idea of what it was all about. They say, you know, every ten years now the amount of knowledge man's got equals *all* the knowledge he had before. Ain't that wicked? Like, when we get to 1980, the knowledge from 1970 to 1980 will be equal to *all* the knowledge up to 1970. How are we gonna deal with it, how are we gonna go with it? No wonder everyone sits bug-eyed in fronta a TV screen, and goes absolutely limp when some jackass is looking at him and sayin, "By Gosh, the Price Is Right." No wonder. There's just no way in the world anyone wants to take a bag of shit and heave it right through one of their own windows for doing it to us. Just lulled into being a buncha slobs and consumers, a buncha people ripe for the plucking, a buncha people that pitchmen can get at any time they want, anyway they want.

I thought one of the biggest insults I'd ever seen at the provincial level in my life hadda be an election in Ontario not too long ago, and they run a picture of a lovely, old rimless-glasses lady sitting there. She was the absolute ultimate, you know, probably someone who was a virgin in her late forties and then married the rector. Geez, there she is thanking the government, you can see the come-to-Jesus look reflected on the lens in her spectacles there, thanking the government for being good enough to send her back a cheque for $372. You know what it was all about, she overpaid them $372 and naturally the sonsofbitches hadda pay her back, and here they are spending the taxpayers' money running an ad telling everyone how good the government is.

That's when you oughta be able to go in and take the paper right off the shelves, throw their typewriters down on the floor, boot them in the arse, and run them right outa town with sticks. But we'll never get there, we're absolutely, we're absolutely lulled right inta just sitting being a bunch of dodos, a buncha middle-class dodos. We all wanna be able to stand on elevators and not talk.

That's the absolute ultimate, to stand like a jackass with five or six other people, looking at numbers up at the ceiling . . . 9,8,7,6. Sooner or later someone cracks a real devastating one like, "Gee, it's a lovely day, ain't it?" Isn't it wonderful? And we have the nerve to laugh at sheep running around going bahhhh.

They ain't learning at all in the schools, no sir. They ain't getting it at all in the schools. They're getting it on the TV and over the radio. Whatever happened to old-fashioned talking. Nowadays it's supposed to be called "communicating." I say it's only because it's in the handsa idiots whose whole idea of communication, as they see it, is to serve their masters. All that means is that they are dedicated to spreading as much bullshit as possible.

I'll give you an idea of how things go, how things is orchestrated from one day to the next . . . all the time. Now, the government in Ottawa's blowing about $300 million on bilingualism. Geez, that reminds me of a story, don't know if I've told it to you or not.

They say they was having a hell of a party at Trudeau's place in the summertime and his little boy, Justin, just as cute as a bug's ear, all dressed up to the nine's, fell inta the pool. By geez, everyone's standing round and no one's doing nothin, and poor little Justin can't swim at all, he's too little. There, all of a sudden Pierre Trudeau, with that wonderful form he showed when he first become PM, he dives in with all his clothes on, he's gotta $500 Perry's of Bloor Street outfit on. Geez, he brings Justin over to the side of the pool, stands him there, the water running off the kid's outfit.

Trudeau, O boys, if looks could kill, finds this big good-looking lifeguard, and he says, "Why the hell did you stand there and not do nothing?" The lifeguard says, "I can't swim Mr. Prime Minister." Trudeau says, "How the hell did you get the job here?" Lifeguard says, "I'm bilingual."

You know, people think all the political jokes is made down in the States. We got some here like Bill 22 in Quebec. Lotta people thought that was some new pope. It wasn't, it was the Quebec Language Bill. That made Trudeau hotter'n a firecracker. Here he's trying to get bilingualism and spending $300 million and his buddy, Bourassa, trying to go in the other direction, he's trying to say one language is the language and the other's nothing. In other words, if you're gonna go on strike in Quebec, and you gotta get a sign, and you're walking up and down, you gotta have your sign in French *and* English, or else you're violating the law . . . that's one of the things they was talking about . . . just carrying it to the extreme. Anyways, Bill 22's been amended: they're calling it Bill 69 and it's designed to put the French tongue back where it belongs. It'll go through lickety split.

I keep asking the question: "Do you think for one second that reporters would ever get off the ground with a Watergate style story in this country?" No way in the world, Buster. Any of them that ever got progress going, their bosses would cut the ground right from under them. All the bosses would be sitting in their homes having phone conversations with this one and that one and they'd be coming into work the next day and they'd short-circuit the goddamn thing to the point where you'd go crazy.

We got our lid on, we got our royal commission way, we got our way of having our ostrich head in the sand like no one's ever seen it. We know how to do it, we know how to hide the body away so no one will ever find it. We're pretty good at that. We're terrific hypocrites, too. How many Canadian trees has been cut down, do you suppose, through the years for newspapers that bullshit the people of Canada about how everything's screwed up in the United States of America? We gotta great country here, but there's lottsa things screwed up. It's awful funny to me that the newspapers don't have the balls to go out and look into anything. Last time they looked into anything was Gerda Munsinger, for goodness sake. That's when poor old Earl Cameron slipped up on The National. I guess it was 1966, the only time I ever heard him make a mistake, he called her Gerda *Moon*singer. Geez, his career musta turned a corner in his wonderful old mind when that happened – Gerda Moonsinger.

She was a lousy carpenter you know, one little screw and the whole cabinet fell apart.

I'd say the last big decision made at CBC . . . as a matter of fact, to get it all in perspective, way back in the Year One, there used to be a song lotta oldtimers will know called "Sheik of Araby."

Now that was the name of the song – it never was the "Shake of Araby," you know what I mean. Then there was Rudolph Valentino, he was in a Hollywood picture called *The Sheik* and I never heard no one, at any time, call it *The Shake*. When you went inta drugstore in Canada and you asked for a box of shakes, they'd have run you out of the place. But all of a sudden the CBC brass decided the word sheik has gotta be pronounced *shake*. Of course, this is one of their two biggest decisions in the last decade. By the way, they trouble-shot that one through and got Lloyd Robertson on "The National" to "shake" this and "shake" that.

Then, of course, after awhile they made their second biggest decision in the decade, that's when they changed shake back to sheik. So help me. God's honest truth. Now, it seems to me that *some* of you might be a mite skeptical bout that story so right here I'm gonna print the memo (pronounced mee-mo, of course) that justified us ginks who've always said sheik when we mean sheik. This here's the memo that got ridda shake:

The word comes from the Arabic *Shaikh* which literally means old man, a title of respect used for leaders of Arab tribes. The pronunciation *shake* is closer to the Arabic than *sheek* and is used by many British people and others who have either lived in or travelled the Middle East. Ever since E. M. Hull's novel and Valentino's subsequent motion picture "The Sheik" the common pronunciation in North America has been *sheek*. All dictionaries prefer this pronunciation to *shake* which some label a Briticism. It is therefore recommended we use the pronunciations *sheek* and *sheekdom*.

J. Rae Office B'cast Language

Now ain't this wicked? Three hundred million a year, over nine thousand people, and two shows in the top thirty made in this country. And do they ever tremble with rage and indignation when you call them on it? No one ever calls them on it, but when you underline it, it's like going to a painter and saying, "I thought you was painting the wall in this room and you missed a great big spot on the wall." Did you ever see the look on his face, did you ever see the way he goes back and gets his roller? O geez, is he ever hotter'n a firecracker.

It's awful hard to know where to begin with people in the broadcasting game. There's all kindsa stories going around nowadays that kinda give you an idea of just where TV is. Course, it don't take a magician to figure out that it's in the grasp of the marketplace boys, I guess you could say the people in the bullshit business. People in government go through the ritual of organizing some statement, generally called a press release . . . thank god we gotta few newspaper boys who don't give a damn what the date is on the press release, they release it if it falls inta their hands.

Broadcasting is really manipulation of the worst kind. There's something awful cynical about it, the way everything is orchestrated and planned. I get a kick out of the way things go from one year to the next. People get away from the old fact that it *ain't* the press that's got a right to know . . . by that I mean the TV, radio, and newspaper boys . . . that *ain't* what it's all about although there's damn few of them who might stop and think about it. It's the public that's gotta right to know.

We live with this religious order called the Liberal Party of Canada that's got some idea of what the public oughta know, and their idea is as damn little as possible, if it's gonna tear the mask off the funny shell game they're playing from one week to the next. So in their own funny way, they've got the press sorta in their minds as the opposition, and they treat it like the opposition. In other words, tell them as little as they need to know, let them go and find out, they don't need to worry too much, cause there's no one with their fingers on the levers of power in the media of Canada trying to find out things. Don't take a goddamn map to explain that one, right?

A lotta people laugh at Trudeau, let them laugh, that's all well and good, he's pretty smart, cause he's seeing through this, he seen through it years ago, so he knows how to make them dance. You take the last election when Dalton Camp predicted we'd have Stanfield as the next prime minister.

The press boys liked Stanfield, they enjoyed his bullshit, they had the time to sit round while he yawned out some kinda explanation. Geez, I always gotta kick outa old Max Ferguson's imitation of Stanfield, that was always terrific, wasn't it? But Trudeau, who the media boys don't like all that much, he keeps them at a distance, he knows how to do that, he keeps them right at a distance. That way there is a nice gap, then when it suits him he gets down to talking to them and they handpick their interviewers.

Anytime he shows up on the TV who's he there with – Patrick Watson, one of his old buddies, having a fireside chat or Bruce Phillips and Carole Taylor, it's all well organized. You don't get in to talk with him on the TV or the radio if you're someone who don't measure up to their standards of what a good man is. Good man, good woman, means someone friendly to us, that's what it's all about. When they're running around Ottawa, they're looking at the whole country, the media, as the enemy. People don't understand that, they don't understand that. Once you're in the bureaucracy government business in Canada, you regard everyone else as the enemy, and you regard anyone as one real hotfire sonofabitch if he's pointing the finger at you. You start screaming, "Not fair, not nice," and, by geez, it don't feel Canadian because we don't have our heads in the sand no more. We can't put on our hats of hypocrisy and walk round with that holier-than-thou superior attitude which really means, we're Canadians, we know how to do it, our shit don't stink, we're Canadians. That's what I get a kick outa.

Boys, when you think of the way they can maneuver and manipulate! I getta kick out of the time that the press got all in a wax over the fact that one time there, Trudeau had given out fifteen interviews to foreign journalists and only five to Canadians. Course, they was mainly radio and TV boys – no Canadian newspaper's got an interview with Trudeau since that last election. There have been a few requests to the prime minister's office but none was granted. O geez, they got upset over that.

It was a funny thing how when you look between the lines, you see Trudeau's press secretary, Peter O'Neill, and you wanna watch all these birds . . . here's this O'Neill saying all kindsa Canadian journalists has been given off-the-record briefings by Trudeau. What is an off-the-record briefing? That's really, "Charlie Lynch, put down your mouth organ and close the door." What that means is, "Charlie, I want you to understand the way we see things from our pulpit . . . " O geez, the vibration in his knickers, being right there, sitting on the throne with the king for a few . . . so from then on he can never turn up with nothing that'll embarrass them, he's in the fold. This is how they maneuver, manipulate, orchestrate, and contrive. They can deny it till the cows come home, but it don't change a thing. *That's* how it works. Freddy Dobbs told you.

You know, radio and TV can be pretty boring, but for some people – like shut-ins – a radio is just about the best friend they got. Justa give you an idea of how important it can be, here's a letter a rabbi friend of mine showed me. Comes from my old stomping grounds.

> Silver Threads Retirement Acres
> R.R. 2,
> Beamsville, Ontario

January 15, 1976

My Dear Rabbi:

I want to thank you very much for your Hanukkah gift of a clock radio. It was just wonderful and very lovely that an absolute stranger like yourself would take time from his holiday season to remember someone like me.

I am 83 years old and have been living here for sixteen years. They treat me very well, but loneliness is sometimes hard to bear. My roommate, Mrs. Zipper, is a very nice person but she is stingy. She has a table radio, but she won't let me use it, and turns it off when I come into the room. Now I have one of my own, thanks to you.

My son and daughter are very nice to me and come to visit once a month. I appreciate it, but I also understand their sense of obligation. This makes your gift all the more wonderful because it was given not from a sense of duty but from a feeling of deep compassion for a fellow human being.

Today, Mrs. Zipper's radio went out of order, and she asked if she could use mine. I told her to go fuck herself.

> I remain yours very truly,
> (Mrs.) Naomi Greenberg

●

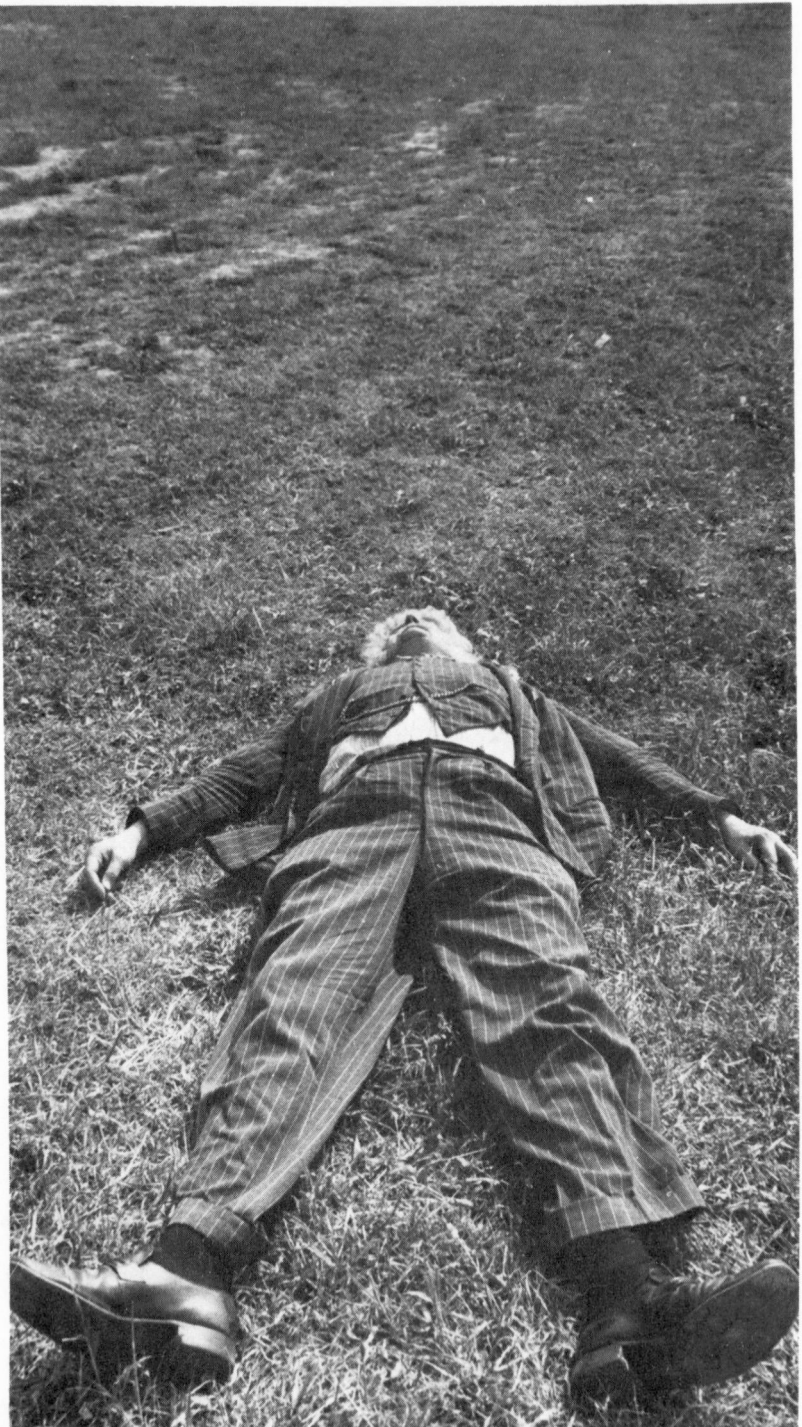

6
The
CBC's Influence
on the
Culture of
Canada

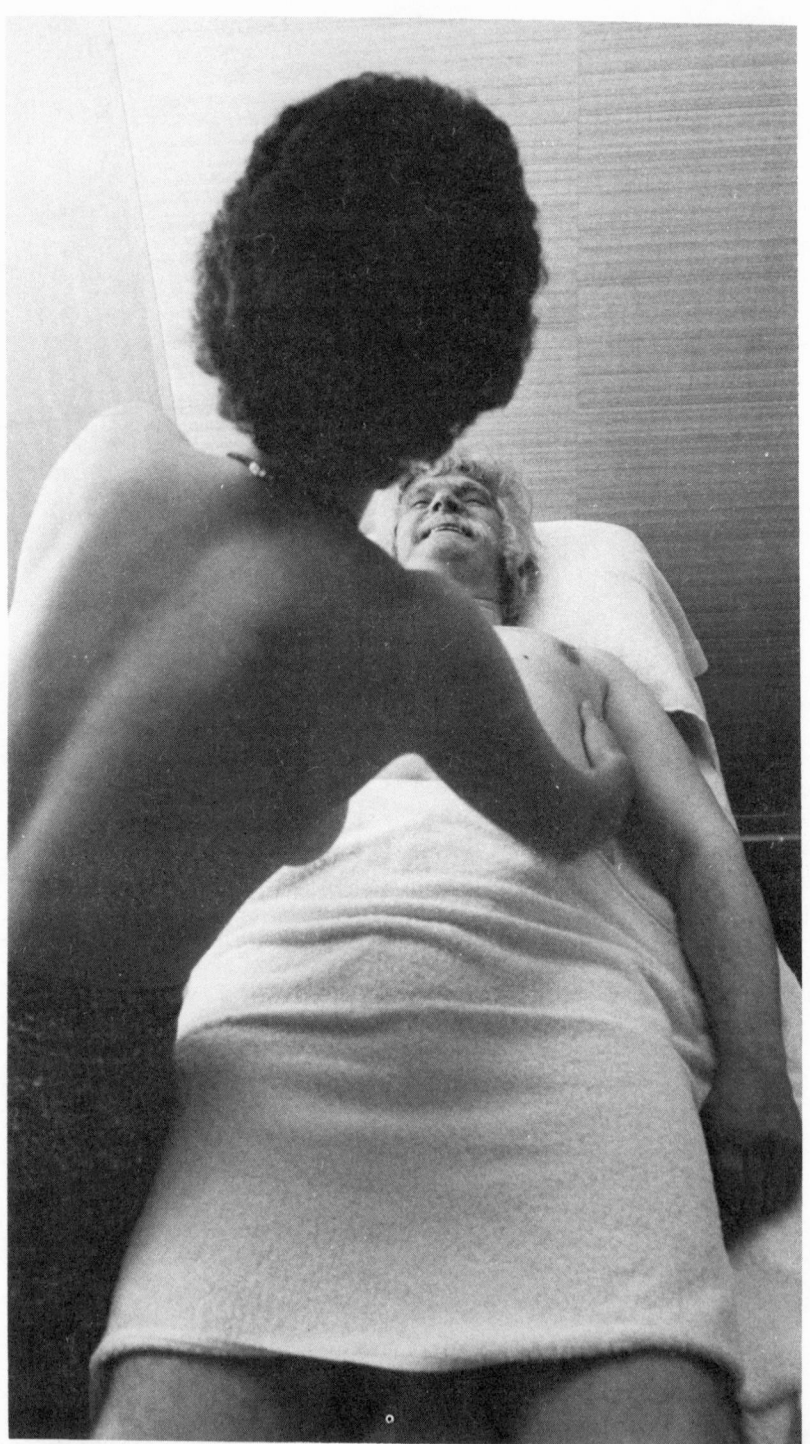

7
How to be Half Pregnant By Pierre Trudeau

I always get a kick outa putting the lamps on the people at speaking engagements, and kinda pausing for effect, and looking all round the hall inta them gleaming clackers looking up at me. It's always fun to point out that I see all the fellows that's trying to lose weight, and I always say to them, "Well you can't felx flab," and that usually gets them. Loosens them up just a little.

When you're on the old rubber-chicken circuit, beating your gums for a dollar in the evenings, they're the best. Not the luncheons. The luncheons, everyone's too sober, but by the time evening comes along, they get pretty liquored up. Canadians have always gone real hairy when there's a bar. Did you ever notice whenever you have your own hospitality, geez you can't drive your last guests out till they've searched your kitchen high and low? Looking for the last drop. It's almost as though they're gonna go only cause there's just no more rye or beer or whatever. It's kinda the Canadian way. In fact, they used to say . . . the Dutch women used to say . . . they always knew our boys cause they always had dirty underwear, and, by geez, could they ever drink beer. It comes from the old tradition, comes from the saying, "Drink up, men, it's closing time."

Mind the old Austin Hotel in Vancouver. Geez, they'd put fifteen to twenty glasses of beer on the table, then shout, "Closing time!" Geez, you hadda nail them down as fast as you could, the mops was pushing at your feet, and then you got out on the street, and like all cities in Canada, they never had any decent public washrooms set up. It's almost as if no one's ever gonna go the bathroom. You search for some of the washrooms in the cities in Canada and, by geez, you'd need a sheriff's posse. Take Toronto, Metropolitan Toronto, with over two million people – they got about six famous stands and that's it. Half the time you're taking your life in your hands going down there.

But by geez, on the rubber-chicken circuit, you're sorta caught in the middle. You're fighting the hospitality-suite guy. He's got keys to the boss's liquor cabinet, and seems to be a big shot, and he'll always go his best lick, and no matter what the hour he'll serve more drinks, and by that time the rubber chicken out in the kitchen's getting cold, and geez, the ice cream's starting to melt, and the *maitre'd* is running around like a one-armed paperhanger in a fit.

By the time they get everyone standing up ready to go, then some jackass moves forward, and proposes a toast to the queen. I've always wondered why her majesty, the queen, could ever be bothered to take any satisfaction, knowing that out here in the colonies, hundreds of men, clean across the country, from St. John's, Newfoundland, to Victoria, British Columbia, is charging their glasses, and saying, "the queen," on a full bladder. It don't make no sense to me.

But then, they sit down, and, by geez, then they'll be ordering the wine that was made yesterday, you know what I mean, never the imported stuff for these dudes, as a rule. By the time they split the shoulders of some Derby, or Château Gai, or whatever it is, boys O boys, they're in great shape to hear the boss's presidential report. And *that* goes on five times longer than it should, cause there's hardly a Canadian businessman that's got the brains to make it short. The only one I know that's got the brains to get up with a one-minute or less speech, the time it takes for one of his colts to run a snappy five furlongs, is George Gardiner. *There's* a fellow that's got the sense to stand up and say what he's gotta say, and then, that's the end of it. I remember the time when old Eddie Taylor said he could never understand symphony music; he thought it went on too long.

When you're on the rubber-chicken circuit sometimes you can hear a pin drop. That's when you can get a moment of real fear. Or, it could be your moment in the sun. I always like to start talking about being a proponent, I guess that's a word I picked up from the business boys, a real bullshit word, sounds great, means nothing. There's always all sortsa people that come to the front to take a bow. Everyone's made a contribution. Don't matter who the hell he is. They've all contributed; some bigger than others.

Take, for example, a groupa one hundred people. They say that sixty five understand the *Bible*. Seventeen get Einstein's theory of relativity. And minus ten get the small print in the North American insurance policy. Of course, they all understand what the guy says when they're all in the kitchen, all gathered round the kitchen table. By geez, when the print comes out, minus ten get the picture. And them salesmen get two bucks off every one they take in. It's just wicked the way that racket goes from one year to the next. All based on fear. (Geez, I just seen a guy in Moose Jaw fling the book inta the garbage can; insurance salesman for sure.)

I kinda like to say that in the golden age of bullshit, we just gotta start laughing at ourselves in Canada. That's the great thing the British have got going for them. Here in the mid-70s, you've got the British giggling their way inta the English channel. Just giggling, and snickering. Spending money like it's going out of style. Grumping away, the way they always done, even in wartime, when the British Tommy was the best grump god ever told the other fellow about. But, they been saying Britain's going to go down for the last time ever since Adam was a little baby.

Somehow, some way, I got a feeling that when the Arabs run into them London banks, with their caftans, and their headpieces, and their white bedsheets on, I think all of a sudden the British banks, just for once, is gonna turn right around and behave just like old Fidel Castro. They're going to say, "Screw off, Buster." That'll be it.

There'll be no way the Arabs will be able to gallop off on their camels with that dough. You see, they're still banking on oil. Despite the fact that they don't have the technology, the British think oil's going to save the day. Well, it ain't. There's just no way in the world it's gonna. They just can't hack it, the way the other outfits in the world can. They went broke trying to show off to the world, trying to make that plane with the French, the Concorde. Most people know that. It's pretty tough to get the black man to lug diamonds outa the ground for the queen or whoever it is. By geez, by the time they've searched his fanny to see if he's got one tucked away, by the time the whites has escaped from Rhodesia with all their valuables on their servants' backs, it's a different situation, isn't it?

I'd like to say . . . I *really* believe . . . if we don't start laughing at ourselves we'll start going down real quick. We'll all pack it in with Trudeauitis, and that's worse'n the burning itch. There'll be nothing to save any of us.

I *love* letting the air out of people's rubbers. By geez, I been a great hit at the Ontario government's sludge-handling and disposal seminars. "Sludge" is an Ontario six-letter word for a well known, world-wide, four-letter word in the English language. They held that meeting out at the Skyline. That's a hotel near the Toronto airport that's still rehearsing . . . a lot are like that.

Then, I was an awful big hit at the Shouldice Surgery Old Boys' Association. That was in the Royal York. Holy doodle, there was over 2,000 graduates of old Dr. Shouldice's Clinic, and he set up examination rooms for all the old boys, and every one of them had to drop their drawers. You couldn't pack a truss at that meeting. I tell you. They was all there, and there was old Freddy Dobbs. That was a fantastic do.

Another time, when I was a real activist, I defeated pay toilets over at the Four Seasons Sheraton. You know, you would've thought that during all the bullshit of International Women's Year, memos, and meetings, and delegates going here, and there . . . What legislation have you got? You would've thought that if any of the provinces would've done anything, they would have taken a lead from one of the states in the US of A, and at least ban pay toilets. Just incredible. We still have discrimination. Of course, her majesty, the queen, put the kibosh on International Women's Year when she told old Sir John Profumo to rise. Boys O boys, after thirteen years of political asylum, there he is, getting the commander of the British empire, and poor old Christine Keeler's still washing dishes. "Rise, Sir John." From what I hear, he never had no trouble getting it up. Wicked altogether. Poor Christine, sitting on a fortune and can't do nothing.

I was turned down as a speaker by the London Life Insurance Company . . . considered too intellectual, by their committee. The British Columbia Breeders' Association, they thought I had a hell of a good act. British Columbia's always been a wonderful place for me, as far as racing goes. We had an awful lotta fun in them days. If anything's happened to modern racing, it's cause, just somehow, some ways the racing world mirrors and reflects the real world we live in.

I can remember the old days, old Norman Fawcett, a funny old trainer in Vancouver. Didn't have a pot to piss in nor a window to throw it out of. But anyways, to humor him along I says to him one day, I says, "How are you doing, Norman?" He says, "O geez, I couldn't buy a safe for hummingbird." There he was, just whistling and laughing on his way to enter one more horse, you could hang your hat on his ribs. He wasn't going to outrun a fat man. But he had hope. That's what racing's all about.

I spoke once at the Golden Quickie at Niagara Falls. It's a home for senior citizens. I had a hell of a fine time there. I remember the time when Boomer Scroggie, my old sidekick, was saying to me, "Fred, you're always shooting your mouth off and boasting. For example, you're claiming you're a fast dresser, cause you can dress in four minutes." And I says, "Well, geez, I think that's quick." He says, "Well what's so quick about it?" And I says, "Well, just try it under a bed at the Morrissey sometime and you'll know pretty darn soon."

I'm *not* a dirty old man. A lotta people say, "O, he's a dirty old man." I prefer to be known as a sexy senior citizen. That way, I can let the air outa people's tires, and that to me, is what's important. I will always operate on the old theory that, "You can't fool old birds with chaff." I've never, ever let school interfere with my education. Especially the kinda school we got nowadays, where the three Rs went out with the dodo. And there's no way I wanna be tabbed as a smart ass cause there's just no way I qualify. A smart ass is a guy who can sit on an icecream cone and tell you what flavor it is.

To get back to what I think we oughta do. We gotta start laughing at ourselves. And I kinda look at myself as an oral editorialist. Now, that sounds pretty sexy in this day and age. Well, with Xavier Hollander selling over ten million books, ain't it funny that we got her finally out of Canada on a shoplifting charge? Boys, that shows you she knew her way round. By the blue geez, did she ever. An oral editorialist is a fellow who's kinda like a newspaper editorial man. He sorta has that wonderful little luxury of having a weewee in a blue serge suit; nobody notices but it's a nice warm feeling.

How do you tell the difference nowadays between fantasy and reality? You find a story coming outa Austria where half the people in the village want to save Hitler's house. Imagine, a movement to save the birthplace of sweet, little Adolf Hitler. The other half wants it torn down and turned into a ten holer. Then, you get a rabbi in Toronto leaving his job and collecting $450,000 severance. It really makes you wonder, cause you know, for sure, that if the Church of England kicked the dean of Toronto out, the only thing they'd do is slap him up on the fanny, give him a bottle of Harvey's Shooting Sherry, and send him up to Orillia, with a one-way ticket on a Gray Coach bus.

But everyone's in showbusiness nowadays. It don't matter if it's the pope, or a rabbi on his way in or on his way out, or Trudeau, or Queen Elizabeth, or anyone. They're all in showbusiness, and I've been on the road myself. There's no two ways about it. Geez, I've worked every place in Canada from Port Matoon, to Souzzum, British Columbia, and I've gone right clean down the Pacific coast from British Columbia, over the line into Washington state, into Oregon, into California. I learned a few things on the way. I learned that a false prophet says only what people wants to hear. Geez, have we ever got a lotta false prophets in Canada. If you wanna be in politics, be a false prophet. You could be a Liberal. You could've been around the last five decades politically in Canada but never call a spade a spade, or a socialist a socialist. You just say you're a Liberal. You can stick in family allowance, baby bonus. Hitler done it in Europe, and Mackenzie King done it in Canada. You give someone a buck for having a baby. Hitler at least had a sexy title for the whole campaign. Way back in the thirties. He called it "Strength Through Joy." By geez, that sounds like something MacLaren's advertising would cook up.

We've had socialism all along. What do you think them crown corporations are – Polysar, and Canadian National, Air Canada, the Canadian Broadcasting Corporation? What do you think that's all about? That's the state mucking around in something. Why are they doing it? Well, as far as I'm concerned, cause some of the business boys never had the balls or the vision, to go into it themselves. Well, sooner or later, it's the same old Canadian story. Finally, the government had to come in and do it. Then, of course, it's a half-assed deal. No two ways about it. I seen a movie last night on the CBC that was so old the girl actually says no.

Nowadays, the quality of life is slipping. Have you noticed? You look at any paper across the country. Could be the *Edmonton Journal,* or the *Vancouver Province,* or the *Halifax This* or *That.* There's the ninety-nine cent funeral advertisements . . . they throw you in a Glad bag and leave you in the driveway.

Winnie was in the supermarket the other day having a look at a couple of tomatoes. They didn't look too good, the Mexican kind you get during the off season, not the home grown ones. The manager, produce manager they call him nowadays . . . it's the Americanization of the English language in Canada. It's been going on ever since Canada started to import football coaches. They're all here, beating their gums every year, starting about . . . when is it,

I guess around about April Fools' Day, they start the football season, don't they? It usually comes in a bit before the hockey grinds to a halt. But there they are going on about *off*ense and *def*ense, two new words from over the border. The produce manager takes the tomatoes over to the scales, sticks them on the scales, comes back and says, "That'll be forty-nine cents, ma'am." Winnie says, "Forty-nine cents for the pair of them?" Manager says, "O no ma'am, forty-nine cents each." She says, "Forty-nine cents *each* for the likes of them? You know what you can do with them." He says, "Well, I already got a seventy-nine cent cucumber up there." You know, if anything ever talks about how the poor consumer has been just tromped on by the supermarket sharks and the food gangsters in Canada, that story tells it all. You don't need to go much further.

Well, how *do* you divorce the fantasy from the reality? How do you get them apart? You got Nixon on the TV a couple of years ago, when he was the president, saying, "I am not a crook." Well, he *was* a crook. You got the Ontario government gonna close down the Doctors' Hospital in Toronto. Six hundred people outa work. All sortsa people who don't know what way up is in the English language. If ever there was an ethnic hospital, it's the Doctors' Hospital in Toronto. Geez, they've got all kindsa young fellows, men and women, working as internes from all over the world. And here's the Ontario government. They send the health minister up to the place, and he says he's gonna close it down, as part of a, "We're gonna save $50 million for the taxpayer." And he didn't even know they had this teaching program in this hospital. Suddenly, thousands of names pour in. Support from all over the place. So all of a sudden they're not gonna close it. So it's back to Nixon. "I'm *not* a crook," when he *is* a crook. The Ontario government, "We're gonna close it down", but, "We'll leave it open," they say.

Or Victor Goldbloom, the guy Bourassa stuck in the Olympics in Montreal, cause Drapeau had made a jackass of himself, as far as the finances and the construction of the stadium and facilities went, so Goldbloom hadda rush in and kinda pinchhit. Geez, he holds a press conference, and says the Olympic site will be ready, but it won't be finished.

Or when we had what become known as the judges' affairs. What an incredible thing. Here you got the three sugar sharks of Canada, charged by the federal government with price fixing, and for eight months they're in court, and there's a guy there by the name of Mr. Justice Mackay. Anyways, he finds them not guilty of the charges that the federal government has brought against them and that's the end of that. An old buddy of his that was in his law firm don't get paid too quick by the government. He sends a bill in to the government for twenty grand, and they say, "Too much. Send another bill." So what does he do? Sends a letter to the *Globe and Mail* and starts claiming that his friend Mackay says that there's all sortsa cabinet ministers ringing up all sortsa judges in Canada. All of a sudden, what we all hear inside the walls of the Toronto Club, the Vancouver Club, the Rideau Club, the St. James Club, and the Manitoba Club, all of a sudden what's going on behind closed doors, is on the front page of the *Globe and Mail*. And now we gotta few judges that's all in a dither cause they have cabinet ministers phoning them up, so we got cabinet ministers on the mat. Geez, we got two, three, four of them . . . three I guess. So what happens after the whole thing's all over? After they appoint someone to look into it? Trudeau says that the cabinet ministers wasn't doing anything illegal. It was just improper. In other words, Trudeau would tell you something like there *is* such a thing as a half-pregnant woman.

Canadians can't think. You get Westons-Loblaws, in 1974, doing $2.7 billion. Not bad for an outfit that manages to manufacture, process, wholesale, and retail. They can nip you at every stage. No wonder they go around saying, "By Gosh, the Price Is Right." And when they get nailed for some little thousand-dollar fine, for some little irregularity, they get in a real snit when someone says, "By Gosh, the Fine Is Right." They don't like to hear that. They *hate* to hear that.

We hear people say that Canadians don't think big, but how can you say that, when you take four cities in the US of A – Dallas, Seattle, New Orleans, and Pontiac, Michigan – that all have one thing in common. They've all got a domed stadium, with a roof on it, and hot and cold running water, and toilets, for men and women. And they say that Canadians don't think big? By god, the stadium they built in Montreal has cost more money than *all* of the others together. And the one in Montreal don't have a roof and not many toilets either.

Course, when it comes to ways of spending the taxpayers' money, you gotta get up pretty early to beat them federal guys. O yeah, the federal guys are the champs. Imagine $200,000 for a washroom survey. A study of washrooms. Washroom habits of Canadians – $200,000. Can't you see it? Who comes in? What'll they do? How many sit down and read? How many write on the wall? Who writes things like "A man without god, is like a fish without a bicycle"? Or "Dracula sucks." Where do we get this stuff? Geez, imagine that. Or what do men do, standing beside one another in a washroom? Do they speak? Or say nothing? If they speak, are they buddies, or if they speak, do they break into fisticuffs? How much paper does so-and-so use? The only thing the stupid damn study found out, that I know of, is that the Irish wash their hands first.

Or take a party costing a quarter of a million dollars, according to the *Toronto Star*, to open the Mirabel Airport. Geez, the Mirabel Airport's such a success, people go all the way to Washington to fly to Paris on the Concorde and make their way back to England. They wanna avoid it so bad. Or go into any library in Canada that Carnegie built for us . . . don't think that Canadians built the libraries in this country, no way. Course, old Carnegie made so much damn money in the United States when he was cutting the swath that he had to give it away. But that's where most of our libraries come from.

Remember Jean Marchand? He's the former member of the Trudeau cabinet that got his driver's license suspended for a year. Anyways, old Jean Marchand . . . Marchand was saying in *Maclean's* that if he was coming to Canada now, there's no way he'd settle in Quebec. He says St. James Bay, the Mirabel, and the Olympic Games projects would be enough to discourage him. Me too.

But geez, we gotta learn to laugh at ourselves. We're coming of age you know. There used to be a time when all the political jokes was brought into the country from somewheres else. Remember the old Casablanca conference joke with Churchill and Eden? There was a whole gang of English and American ginks, two dozen maybe, sitting around the conference table there and Eden sends a note round to Churchill saying, "Beg your pardon, sir, but your fly is open." Well, old Winnie . . . boys, you hadda get up pretty early in the morning to whip the likes of him. Maybe only Lloyd George could outtalk him. He was a hell of a showman, never stuck for an answer. He always knew what to say. He whipped a note right back to Eden that said "Fear not, Anthony, for an old bird never falls from his nest."

It's like the Ontario Hospital Insurance Plan. OHIP the people of Ontario call it. There's this old couple, they go to see their doctor. They tell him that what they want to do is to make love, right there on his table, right in front of him, cause they want his assessment of things. Well, like all doctors he says, "Take your clothes off," and he goes out, then comes back, and they're going at it. And after everything's all over, he says, "As far as I'm concerned, you're fine. Put your clothes on, I'll see you in my office."

Doctors are the greatest ones for saying, "Take your clothes off, put your clothes on." A real kinda mechanical way of doing things. Old Winnie says there's nothing like lying down on one of their tables and, oh geez, does she ever hate that. She says with your legs all strapped into them stirrups, and them looking at you, and then they start talking about how their stocks is doing or something.

Anyways, the couple says, "Can we come back next week? We figure we oughta have a examination every week for, O, about a month." The doctor says, "If that's what you wanna do, that's all right with me." So, they're back again, they go at it, he says it's okay, you're real lucky, you two people, you seem to be real healthy, put your clothes on. Same deal the next week, and the week after.

Finally the doctor says, "Listen here, you're both doing wonderful. Just wonderful. I can't complain about either one of you. As far as I can see, you're both real lucky. Everything seems to be working real good. Now come on into my office, I wanna talk to you." Well, they put their clothes on, go into his office, and the doctor says, "What the hell is this all about?" "Well," the guy says, "I'll tell you. I'm married, she can't come to my place. She's married so I can't go to her place. We go to the Royal York it's going to cost $46 a night. We go to the Skyline it's $34. You charge $10, and we get $9 back from OHIP."

So you see, it kinda shows that we're coming of age.

Actually, old Nixon, he done for politics what the Boston Strangler done for door-to-door salesmen. There used to be some pretty good jokes about Nixon around the time of Watergate. I swiped mosta mine from the *New York Times*. I remember one. Ever heard of Watergate deodorant? It don't stop the smell none, but it sure shifts the blame. That was a pretty good one.

Then, the two fellows who met one dark night in Washington, and one says to the other, "What are you doing, Bill?" Bill says, "Well, don't let on to my mother, but I'm working for Nixon." The guy says, "I didn't know that. Why don't you want your mother to know?" Bill says, "Well she thinks I'm playing piano in a whorehouse."

But you know, Nixon's not the only president to have a crooked vice-president. Eisenhower had one too. And if Nixon had been captain of the *Titanic* . . . talk about Churchill being good with the gift of the gab . . . geez, Nixon would've told everyone that they'd just stopped for ice.

But I get a kick outa that joke that was going round Ottawa where they was talking about bilingualism costing us $300 million according to Keith Spicer, who runs around smiling about it, from one enda the country to the next. As far as I'm concerned, the whole bilingualism exercise, the way it's been explained to me, was designed for this purpose and this purpose alone: They was awful afraid, the Ottawa Liberals, that the intellectuals in Quebec would not come to the federal cause. They was awful afraid they was gonna go with René Leveque and the Parti Québecois. So they wanted to kinda give them an environment to work in, they wanted them to hook their wagon to the federal Liberal star. So bilingualism was kinda the whole groundwork that was laid to sorta lure them outa Quebec and get them inta the mainstream of

Ottawa. You get the idea? They know damn well there's no way you're gonna teach old dogs new tricks. They knew darn well that thousands of civil servants will run off to learn French if you waste the money, and the other way round. They was never under any delusion. But that was the real idea behind the plan. That's so. Geez, we've got some smart buggers up there. I would never've given anyone credit to cook something up as good as that.

Have I told you the one about the uplift and Pierre and Margaret going to the parliament buildings? Well, Pierre told Margaret that it would be a good idea if she turned out early in the morning, so there they are, by gosh, she's a real knockout. Just a terrific looking woman, you know. And they're walking along a couple of blocks away from the parliament buildings, and all of a sudden he starts picking on her, starts talking at her, gets a spell on. No sooner'n he gets going, he says to her, "You know, Margaret, I don't think you're wearing any uplift there." Geez, she glares at him, and he says, "Well, come on now, I don't think you've got a brassiere on." She says, "Look here, Pierre, I'm a darn good looking woman, least you used to think so. Now you stop picking on me. You told me you wanted me to turn out early this morning, so you back off."

Well, he shrugs his shoulders, don't say nothing, and they go along, neither one saying nothing to the other, and after another block he says, "You know, Margaret, I've been looking at that skirt you're wearing, and it's a little short. You used to be awful sharp on fashions. You always said I knew something about it too, and now I don't know. By gosh, I'm wondering why you'd have something on like that." She says, "Look, I got good looking legs, I'm proud of the way I look. Now you have a spell on today, so you just back right off and stop being foolish."

Well, he shrugs his shoulders, they get to the steps, a gust of wind lifts her skirts up. By geez, Pierre barks at her, "Margaret, I don't think you got anything on underneath there." She wheels round, looks him right in the eye and says, "Look, Pierre, it's your arse they're after, not mine."

Well, you know, gambling's a favorite pasttime of mine and I'd like to tell you some gambling stories. There's this old couple . . .

well, not that old . . . but they had a lotta mileage on them. They left Calgary and shipped out to Las Vegas to kinda play the tables and have a bitta fun. Each night they used to meet in their room before heading out. He'd go his way and she'd go hers.

He had no luck at all: he went to the crap table and every time he got the dice, colder'n a mackerel, up would come big Dick or snakeyes. Geez, he was there twenty minutes, they cleaned him out. Back to the room he goes, turns on the TV, there's nothing he wants to see. He's feeling real sorry for himself, but then he's trying to shrug it off and make out he's a sport, but his shorts is burning.

Anyways, he finally orders up a sandwich and a drink, has that, then has a shower, and goes to bed early, tosses and turns, keeps looking at the clock. Finally, he has to admit to himself he's sitting there wondering where in hell is she? It's twelve o'clock, one o'clock. Four o'clock there's a sound of a key in the lock on the door, and in she comes, just a laughing and agiggling, higher'n a kite. O, is she ever chuckling, she's got a great big mink coat on. And she says "What happened to you, honey? No luck? You've got a face on you like a torn-over shoe." "Well," he says, "I didn't have no luck at all. Where did you get that coat?" She says, "I won it playing bingo. You oughta try bingo." "Bingo," he says. "Yes."

Well, out they go the next night. He goes his way, she goes hers. This time he tries the old cards, you know, twenty-one, blackjack. He don't get nothing, he's cleaned out before you can say Jack Robinson. Same thing happens. He goes back to the room, tosses and turns after having some grub, trying the TV, having a shower. She comes in around 4:30 in the morning, got the mink coat on and a big setta pearls. Same thing. She says, "No luck, honey?" He says, "None at all," and he says, "Where'd you get them?" She says "Them pearls? Well, I got them playing bingo."

Well, by gosh, the next night, about an hour before they gotta go home . . . he says, "Listen," he says, "Honey, I'm running a bath for you." She says, "Thanks a lot, dear." She finally goes into the bathroom. She says, "Dear, you forgot to put the plug in." He says, "No I didn't, honey. I didn't want you to get your bingo card wet."

I always getta kick out of that story, and it reminds me of just one more. And that's the time the fellow goes into the bank, this is in Winnipeg, and he looks like the last of the big-time spenders. Opens up an account, puts two thousand bucks in it, and he's in there every single day about the same time putting two thousand bucks inta his account. Well, the assistant manager, a little toady type, runs up to him all smiles, his clackers gleaming, "How would you like to meet the manager?" he says.

Well, this fellow's got a deadpan on his face, his map's real turned off. He says, "Well, if you want me to meet him, I'll meet him. It don't matter to me." "Well," the toady says, "He'd really like to meet you, you're a real good customer."

Well, the next day he's in there, another two thousand dollar deposit. He goes in to meet the manager, and the manager's all smiles, and rubs his hands. He says, "By geez, sit down. What is it, if you don't mind my asking, just what is it you do for a living?" "Well," the fellow says, "I don't mind your asking. I'm a gambler." "O," says the manager, lying through his teeth, "Ain't that wonderful."

You know, you can just see it, "ain't that wonderful," what a . . . imagine going to a bank manager and saying, "I'm a gambler, I want a loan." You know they're the kinda fellows . . . who said it, I forget who said it . . . they'll give you an umbrella when the sun's shining and grab it off you as soon as it starts to rain.

Anyways, there's the fellow saying he's a gambler, and he says, "As a matter of fact, I win two thousand bucks every time I make a bet, it don't matter what it is. Cards, horses, dice, you name it. I'll bet you two thousand bucks you've only got one ball." Geez, the manager's sitting there hiding behind his desk the way most businessmen do, and looks down in his lap, looks up with a kinda twinkle in his eyes, and he says, "Well, I've got a bit of inside information." Then he flashes a smile with the old clackers. The gambler says, "Okay. Let's verify it in a week. Is that fair?" "Sure enough," says the manager. So, the gambler goes out.

The deposits continue, two thousand bucks like clockwork every day, and then, when the week goes by, he comes back to the manager's office. This time the manager's all business and says, "Close the door, close the door." So, the gambler closes the door.

The manager says, "Now let's go over this again. You bet me two thousand dollars I've only got one ball, and you say you never lose a bet. You always make two thousand when you bet?" The gambler says, "That's absolutely correct. Now let's verify it."

So, the manager gets up from behind the desk where he's been hiding, comes out, takes his trousers down, by geez, he's standing there with a pair of salmon-pink crotch huggers on, looking like an absolute jackass. So he takes them off, and the gambler goes over and gives the old army short-arm inspection. Just as he's doing that, the door opens and in comes the assistant manager, who faints dead away. "Geez," the bank manager says, "what in hell's the matter with him?" The gambler says, "I don't know. I just bet him four thousand I'd have you by the balls in forty seconds." ●

8
The Horses Study Long, Study Wrong

By geez, if you're gonna talk about horseracing, seems to me the one thing you gotta talk about first and foremost is the most forgotten thing of all in horseracing, and that, of course, is the horse.

Sure makes my blood boil when I turn on the likes of Johnny Carson some night and he's got Willie Shoemaker sitting there, one of North America's leading jockeys. They're going on, beating their gums, about how dumb the horse is. O geez, does that ever get me hot in a hurry when I see them two going on about how stupid the horse is. Shows you the power of the tube, don't it? Soon as something goes out on the tube that's it, it's just about law, you know. "The Price Is Right," "It's Mainly Because of the Meat," Mr. Price and Mr. Pride, and all the other slogans you can think of.

I'm gonna ask a question. Is the horse all that dumb? cause I think that's what we gotta zero in on. I suppose if you wanna say in view of the people that raise them, and own them, and race them, and ride them, and bet on them, the horse is dumb from the standpoint of being the object of their attention. If the horses could all rise up, there's one thing for goddamn sure – they'd never all sit in the damn grandstand and bet on human beings. No way in the world they'd ever bother with that.

I've always taken exception to that particular hypothesis and I wanna beat my gums for a few seconds cause I think it's awful important.

First of all, let's say it's a hot summer's day. Could be in the Fraser Valley, the Annapolis Valley, could be on Tony Zeigler's farm south of Edmonton, Alberta. There's two horses standing in a field. Now, why do you think horses stand head to tail? You ever noticed that? Yeah, they line up, side by side, each one's got his rump opposite the other's head. Now, why would they do that? It's so's each one can act as a fly swatter for the other, swishing his tail and clearing the damn flies from the other's face. Would you say they're absolutely stupid if they do that? Do you think they talk to one another? No way. Now, is it a dumb animal that does that? Not to my way of thinking.

Let's take a buncha horses standing in a field. Most of the time, they got an itch they can scratch it themselves with their hooves or their teeth, get the idea? Course, they get an itch they can't reach, they can rub up against a tree. Now there are still some parts they might not be able to get ahold of. So what do you think they do? What would we do in a similar situation? We'd go over to the old ball-and-chain and say, "Honey, would you reach up and scratch me in such-and-such a place?" Well the horse does the same thing by touching another horse on the spot that's itchy and the other horse, as sure as I'm standing here . . . god's honest truth, strike me dead if I'm lying . . . the other horse'll respond by rubbing that very spot. Now, is that a dumb animal that'll do that? Not to my way of thinking.

O, there's all kindsa things you could say. During the wartime when the bombs was falling on the horses, after the first impact they just stood in their stalls like little majors and never bothered;

they knew if they was going to get hit they'd get hit, no use making a fuss. You could go to Stampede Park in Calgary, used to be called Victoria Park Racetrack, right where the Elbow meets the Bow. Geez, they had a fireworks display the night after the Stampede you'd think World War III was breaking out. Four to six hundred horses stabled right there in the barns, never turned a hair, they knew they wasn't going to be hurt by that. Is that a stupid, neurotic animal? Standing there with fireworks that was scaring shit outa half the audience? Now, a dog for example, if he's around when bombs is falling or lightning or thundering, knocking down trees, dogs and wolves being the same thing, being creatures of the forest, know when they gotta get moving. Horses never grew up or lived there. They grew up on the plains, they're not frightened by the same things. Fact is, a horse'll lie right down in the rain, don't bother him none at all.

I can't think of a subject that's occupied my time and kinda grabbed me right by the bag like horseracing has. I don't know rightly what it's all about. Can't be to get something for nothing for as old Damon Runyan wrote after his sixtieth coffee, "All horseplayers die broke." It's a hard subject to come at. People say to me, "Fred, can you make any money betting on it?" I'm talking about thoroughbreds, I'm not talking about Brand X, the standard-breds, I'm talking about racehorses. They all stem from three old stallions that was brought to England with the funniest names you ever heard of: the Darley Arabian, the Byerley Turk, and the Godolphin Barb. Brought by some opportunistic Englishmen from the Middle East, not looking for oil in them days, looking for horses and presents to bring back. This was back in the days of King James I and Charles I.

Geez, them was the days when the king of England wasn't afraid of no one. Used to send his couriers right into the churches of England, right down the aisle, slick and clean right up to the pulpit, and they'd hand the damned royal order to the archbishop, and he'd have to read it out to the congregation: "His majesty the king requests that everyone attend the race meet at one o'clock on York Heath . . ." or whatever.

You know, in the old days, the boys started up racing in England with what they called the Jockey Club. What a funny outfit that was. Did you ever stop to think what a funny thing . . . you know, like the Oxford library in England at Oxford University, some of the worst thieves that ever trod the roads of England donated dough to it cause it was the thing to do. The British has always been smart, you know, they never did turn their nose up at a loose pound, they'd stick it in and buy a shelf of books.

But, boys O boys, what a buncha sonsofbitches them original Jockey Clubbers was. Lotta stories about them, you know. The early membership of the club consisted of about a hundred men . . . no women, of course . . . well, they was the honorary and honorable directors as they called themselves, which governed . . . I guess you'd say paternally and certainly firmly. All the business of what could best be described as the British turf. O, they was all powerful. As a matter of fact, in them days when they first got going they warned off . . . "ruled off" as we say here in North America . . . the prince regent, "first gentleman of the land," because of a little caper by a jockey, bird name of Chifney and a horse name of Escape. Of course, the prince backs his man up . . . not like the people we have nowadays in Canada who run for cover when a subordinate's in the shit, they don't want to be covered with it too.

So the prince claims his jockey is innocent of whatever caper it is the Jockey Club has lowered on Chifney. In fact, the club charged that Chifney had been making money on the side with the prince's horses, illegal like. So, the prince defends his guy and the Jockey Club brass makes the charge stick against Chifney. The prince *has* to accept the ruling, that's how powerful they was, and he does it with a great deal of dignity as befits a man of royal blood. The directors told the prince, "We don't like the look of what was going on in that last ride by Chifney on Escape . . . your horse, you're responsible . . . OUT!" Well, that gives you some idea of who these birds was.

One bird who comes to mind who was no slouch was Sir John Lade. He was an amateur coachman, wealthy young man, his ancestors was a bunch of brewers and he was a friend of the prince regent. Actually, he married a good-looking dish who was the

mistress, so they said, of a highwayman named Sixteen String Jack
. . . married his mistress! That, of course, was when old Sixteen
String was suffering at Tyburn . . . hope I don't have to draw you
a map of what kinda place Tyburn was, he was there for the rest of
his natural born. Anyways, this Sir John Lake never took a back
seat when it come to taking a wager and he made one with a
well-known high roller name of Lord Cholmondeley.

Now, of course, Sir John was a lightweight and Cholmondeley
was a welter, nevertheless, Sir John backed himself at Brighton to
carry Cholmondeley piggyback twice around the Steyne. The story
got all around Brighton and, geez, every woman who had anything
to show turned out, sitting there in her coach, lining the racecourse.
It was the biggest moment of theatre they'd had there, down on
the channel, for two decades.

Cholmondeley shows up and Sir John demands that the peer
strip right down to the bare pole. Cholmondeley says, "Strip? What
the devil's nonsense is this?" And the baronet coolly says, "Well, I
bet that I'd carry *you*, not that I'd carry you and your clothes, so
take them off!" Well, by geez, Cholmondeley didn't want to cut
the mustard no more, and he backed off the bet right on the spot.
Well, that'll give you an idea of the sorta birds they had running
the Jockey Club in them days. Course, what would you have done
if you was Cholmondeley with ten thousand of the bluest and
best-looking eyes in England looking at you? You gonna show your
old tellywhacker to a crowd like that just to win a bet? No
goddamn way.

I don't know how you can best describe what you want out of a
horse, but I remember an old horse trainer name of Harry Ord and
geez, he had an awful time getting a license. This was out at the
old Lansdowne Park on Lulu Island in Vancouver. Geez, Harry
come outa the cookhouse one morning and seen a whole lotta
horsemen trying to form a circle around a small horse van. There
was a fellow trying to load a horse. By geez, a stick of dynamite
wouldn't've got that sonofabitch into that van, there was just no
goddamn way he was gonna go, he dug his forelegs right in, he
wasn't gonna budge.

So Harry comes up . . . he was never a fellow you could say was skilled in the art of public relations . . . and in a loud voice he said, "You sonsofbitches make me laugh. You know how many stupid parts there is to the engines of the cars you drive, but not one of you knows how many bones there is in a horse's body."

Well sir, you could hear a pin drop.

Harry walks up to the horse, says to the fellow who's holding the horse, "Give me that halter shank that was on the horse." Then he says to the fellow, "Now, have you got some rope?" Guy says, "I got some in the cab." Harry says, "Well, go and get it." Guy comes back with about fifteen feet of rope. Harry loops it through the halter, takes it along the side of the horse to his arse and up back round again. Walks up the ramp of the van, clucks to the horse, walks into the van and the horse follows him right in like a little major.

Geez, they stood there with their goddamned jaws dropped. And Harry, at that time, couldn't get a license. Couldn't get anyone to endorse his application. Well, he didn't give a damn. He says to me one day, he says, "Fred, if you're gonna buy a horse, you wanna look for five things: it's what you call the Five Bs - breeding, bones, brawn, brains, and balls." And I kinda got a kick outa that cause time and again the horsemen on this continent just don't have patience with a young horse, whether it's a yearling that he's breaking and showing the ropes to, or a two-year-old that he's actually starting out to train. Most of the time the answer is, "Let's lop his plumbs off and when we do that he'll be a nice little gentleman." To me, it's a kinda cop out. Any horseman'd lop off a horse's jewels should have the same operation performed on himself. That'd put an end to that practice. You bet.

There's another funny thing that goes on in North American racing along with a whole lotta other things that make no sense, and that's the thing called "bucked shins." It's not a condition you hear about in Britain or France . . . funny thing, you know, where they invented modern thoroughbred horseracing, in England, you don't hear about it there hardly at all. It's all over North America. I've heard horsemen says, "O, it's kinda like a charlie horse in a human being." Other people say: "It's sorta like a young ballet dancer, being put on point too soon by a teacher who's conning her parents." But it's worse than that. It's stress . . . S-T-R-E-S-S . . . right on the shins and you can see it. When you do an autopsy on a horse that's kicked the bucket, you get right down to the bone, you can see the stress right there. That's nature's way of saying, "Slow down, Buster." When a horse is suffering from this condition, a lot of horsemen ain't above freezing their shins so they won't feel no pain and then still running them which is the *stupidest* thing anyone could ever do.

You know, when a horse is bucking, or about to, his shins is mighty sore. The moment you go in a stall and put your hands forward to touch him, he backs right up. He's sore, you're darn right he is, and he don't want no part of your hands on him at all. Back right away, he's saying, "Geez, don't touch that, it hurts."

When you think about racing in this country, so often you've got to go back to England where they kinda got a scholarly approach to things. For example, they've put out a paper in England called *Sporting Times* . . . O geez, been round for seems like centuries. And in them days, you know, you could . . . if you was writing racing, you never needed to worry about anyone's sensitivity the way you do now. They didn't have the libel laws that protect all sortsa people up to all kinds of shenanigans nowadays.

In them days, in something like *Sporting Life* they write . . . right *there*, in the paper, "We have before had occasion to compliment the sagacity and intelligence displayed by Mr. So-and-So's horses. They never win when they are favorites but always when long odds is to be obtained about them. The public oughta be grateful to them." And then they might go on to say, "So-and-So was a heavy favorite because of the past history of the horses from this particular barn it was a dead certainty that the horse would be nowhere. So-and-So run so badly at Newmarket that it was inconceivable that he should have won at Nottingham." And I've seen in print, in *Sporting Life*, sentences like this: "If So-and-So had been allowed to run with her head loose, she must have beaten him."

Course, the racing writers in them days would write to the great dictator of the English Jockey Club, Admiral Rouse, and they'd direct their attention to him and they'd say, "We trust the admiral

has taken note of these and other performances at Nottingham."
Well, you'll never get that stuff now. No way in the world. Poor
old horseplayer's the ham in the sandwich nowadays. And there's
just no one who's gonna be able to go to bat for him. Even if a
young racing writer wanted to write some stuff he'd be stopped by
the editor who usually goes to the parties the racing boys throw
every year. So that kinda shows you something about the golden
age of bullshit, taking one tiny, unimportant subject. I'm saying
that in deference to most people; to me it's *real* important.

I was thinking about old Frank Merrill Jr., the top trainer in
America three times, coming out of . . . I think it was Brampton,
Ontario, or Brantford. Advised by his doctor when he had
tuberculosis to work outside. Merrill finally . . . big comic, you
know, would get down on his knees in a stall, with a horse, put his
hands out and look up at you when you was watching . . . *loved* an
audience . . . then shake his hands, and freeze, and say, 'Heel'."

By geez, he knew more about looking after a sore horse than
most vets could ever dream of. Mind one time, I asked Frank how
a horse was doing, and he said, "O geez, Fred, don't touch him." I
says, "Why not?" He says, "He's sorer than a wedding prick."

Frank once says, and I'll never forget it, he says, "If the
do-gooders of this nation really got their way and closed down all
the tracks, the real harm that would come of it, we'd have to open
hundreds of mental homes, right slick and clean across the country
to look after all the people who've got the horseracing habit." I
think there's a lotta truth in that, so for every sonofabitch who goes
around the bend and maybe bets the pay cheque, or the last buck,
or the welfare cheque, or whatever . . . and there's thousands of
them . . . O geez, they'd be in pretty poor shape if the tracks was
closed.

One of the funniest old characters I ever heard about in
Canadian racing was old Jack "Chattahoochee" Smith. Finally died
in an old men's home in Calgary. He was well looked after by Lee
Williams, an Edmonton businessman, got a real kick outa him . . .
real kind to Jack in the final days . . . old Jack was well looked
after.

Jack was really a barber by trade in Calgary, raced a few horses,

done so for many a decade. He'd spit on his hands when he was
cutting your hair, and then reach down and rub his shoes when you
wasn't looking, and then he'd say to you, "Do you want a wash?"
Most fellows in a barbershop, or hair stylist, as they call them
nowadays, will say, "O, I'll wash it tonight." It's kinda like a guy
going into buy a new setta clothes and he's got an *avoirdupois* on
him like the Aga Khan but he always says, "O, I'm losing weight so
you don't have to go by that measurement." Most fellows wanna
cheat the barber outa a hair wash, and, geez, Jack'd rub his hands
through the fellow's hair and then he'd show his hand and say,
"Geez, I think you could do with a wash there, and maybe a
shave." He was a pretty sharp old fellow, Jack.

He had a small stable of what you'd call real hard knocking
horses on the half-mile tracks of the prairie, you know. His best
mare was one name of Chattahoochee, named after a river down in
the states on the border of Georgia and Alabama. He was talking to
me, one time, about her, and he says, "You know, Fred, the only
time they ever got her beat was when they got her down on the rail
and put her in jail and wouldn't let her out. By the time she started
moving it was too late." Most of the time she'd skim around them
short lanes and tight turns like a hoop round a barrel, could hang
right on the wood there and just scamper.

Jack also had a mare name of Pancake Mary, and by geez, if you
went out and spit on the track she'd step up twenty lengths, she
loved the mud.

Jack always used to say, "The thing that gets horses is love, care,
and kindness." Old Chattahoochee'd get into the Crown Royal –
Royal Crown, as he'd call it – sitting on a bale of hay in his tack
room, late at night, and he'd start reciting, and he'd say, "Did you
ever see a cat waiting for a mouse to come outa the hole? I'm like
the cat, I can sit back and wait for a long time. I can wait for a spot
for one of my horses. I mind the time I walked Carhan King in
Winnipeg for twenty-eight days. I told the jock, 'He's sharp now,
he's higher than a kite. You just sit back in fourth hole, there, first
time around, then just set sail for the front. It'll just be like picking
cherries off a tree.'

"If you put a good bed under a horse," old Chattahoochee used to say, "he'll run a whole lot better for you." He wasn't above telling you some of his tricks. Once he bored a hole in his tack room. There was a rich outfit with a feed room on the other side of the partition. By geez, he got his hand in and outa their bran sacks every night soon as they was on their way home. Sharp old horseman.

He used to say he always knew that a horse looked good when he had his tail up over his back like a fantail pigeon. He'd say. "If you're ever sitting in the grandstand, you can throw your old *Racing Form* out, forget all the knowledge you've ever had, forget all your history of racing, just have a look at them as they're on their way to the post. You ever see one with his tail up over his back like a fantail pigeon, you get right down to the wickets and get your money down on that baby – he's feeling good."

Course, Chattahoochee's advice don't take care of the sonsofbitches that's sound asleep on parade. I mind the time I seen a horse name of Windy Sea standing sound asleep in his stall in the paddock at Santa Anita Park in Arcadia, California. His trainer, Cecil Jolley, came round after checking one of his hooves and seen him asleep and give him a jab in the shoulders with his thumb. By geez, the son of a buck went out and run in 1:09 flat for the six furlongs, win by five. So talk about relaxing before a race, eh?

Poor old Jack Smith, you know, got so upset that he . . . old Jack used to use the phrase, "He's as fit as human hands can make him." He loved saying he had a sharp long shot he was gonna release deep down in the brine barrel. And he'd come along in the morning joking, saying, "O by geez, smart boys paid the feed bills on this one, you know." O, he was a lot of fun, Jack was.

One time, I mind, he win a race and he win it easy, and he was so excited he pissed himself right in the winner's circle. Well, the stewards had to take action – in racing, they want some kinda phrase to describe whatever the trouble is, they say, "for conduct not in the best interests of racing." Fined poor old Jack fifty bucks.

Was he ever a superstitious sonofagun, if you ever had a camera or anything like that, geez, he'd say, "I'm not gonna win now." It'd just take the bloom off the rose for him, he'd be spooked as soon as he seen you just about to take a picture.

I want to tell you a little bit about old Jim Speers from Winnipeg who owned the Whittier Park Stock Farms at Carberry, Manitoba. He was really "Mr. Racing" in western Canada. I remember one time he was about to start a race meet in Calgary and the horsemen went on strike, said the purses wasn't good enough. By geez, Speers went out to the airport, hired a plane to Vancouver, and borrowed fifty thousand bucks from Austin Taylor, flew back, said, "Okay boys, I got the money, let's race." They don't have many men like that in Canada no more.

He was the guy who coined the phrase, "There's a little bit of larceny in all of us and it'll come out at the race track." Matter of fact, Speers started the daily double, you have to pick the winners of the first race and the second race to cash in, started it in Calgary, Alberta. That's a Canadian invention not many people know about.

Lotta people don't know what parimutuel betting means. It really started in Paris, France. Course you know that the French pronounce Paris as *"Paree."* Guy name of Pierre Ollet, got sick, sore, and tired of the odds the bookmakers was laying on the horses. So he says, "If I take my hat off, and all you guys put your money in it, I'll just charge you a little percentage of what you're betting for handling the transaction, and what I'll do is, I'll pay all the winners all the losers' money." So that's how come we get the name parimutuel.

Nowadays, of course, the parimutuel system of betting is hooked into something the horseplayer calls a tote board. Name comes from the American Totalisator Company which has a machine which is a kinda giant adding machine. You have win, place, show betting in various denominations – two, five, ten, twenty, fifty, hundred dollars. All the tote board is, is a collection of adding machines feeding into one big adding machine. Every ninety seconds, when the machines have added up how much money's bet on each horse in each category, the machines compute the odds for the total at that time and it all flashes up on a board set up in the infield. Sos the horseplayer in the stands is getting a ninety second-by-ninety second updating on how the action's going.

It's a funny thing. On a racecourse you can tell a man his wife's no good, you can tell him mistress's no good, but don't *ever* tell him his horse is no good. Yet the same dang people'll pay slave wages for what I'd call paid slaves, to trot around their horses, around their barns. And on big days . . . like in Canada where we have the Canadian International Championship closing day at the Woodbine autumn meet.

I mind the time I went out to Drumtop's stall. She was a good mare up from New York, one of the best in the United States. I was just moseying around to pass the time of day, there was no one there, the stall door was open, and she was there looking out. I could've slipped her a slow pill or done whatever I wanted. No one there guarding her at all. Horse worth half a million dollars. Going to run that afternoon in a big race. Now, would you leave a diamond or some kinda gem in a shop window where anyone could reach in? No way in the world. It just astonishes me. I'm actually amazed they don't have more weird things happening. And, by geez, there's been some really weird things happen in racing.

Mind the time a horse name of Lid win a race at the old Blue Bonnets track in Montreal. That was back in the days when they used to have horse painters. Geez, Lid came inta the winner's circle . . . O, what a lovely looking bay he was. One of those funny times when all of a sudden, without any warning at all, and despite the sunshine, it starts to rain. Well, it don't rain more'n a minute and all of a sudden Lid's changing color from a bay to a gray. All around him is this funny brown dye on the ground. Course, one of the painter's had gone to work on him and touched him up the night before they shipped in.

Course, many's a fellow used to run a ringer. They say in the days that Al Capone run the old Sportsman's Park track in Cicero, Illinois, he pretty well had everyone in his hip pocket. Geez, in them days you never knew what was going on. And there was a fellow name of Ralph Cooper, horseman out of Saskatchewan, who owned a pretty good mare named Lover's Lass. She was a real bullringer, could run around the half-mile track, O geez, she was good and she was awful good early in the year . . . if she run fresh she was real dangerous.

Cooper had in mind to make a killing one year. So, instead of racing Lover's Lass the next year on the western circuit, he decided to have her "fired" over the winter and then turned out to pasture so that the firing could heal and then put her inta training. "Firing" is when you take a thing kinda like a waffle iron, and you attach it to all of the inflamed part of the ankle; the idea is that the pus comes out of the holes you burn in, then a scab forms and it's clean and the whole injury can heal. Well, Cooper had one of the best vets out in California do the job on her. She went back to the farm on the prairie and didn't go into the races at Calgary, Edmonton, Regina, Saskatoon, Winnipeg, just stayed on the farm. Finally, they put her in training and they shipped her to Chicago for the racing at the half-mile Sportman's Park.

By geez, Cooper checks into the Stevens, the biggest hotel in the world, now the Hilton Stevens. The next morning he goes out and plays a feeble kinda game with himself, looks at every store front along the street in Cicero and decides which one's a bookmaker, which ain't. Goes in and puts a little money down here, a little money down there. After a few hours he's got himself a nice bet. Goes out to the track that afternoon, he's got Paul Bailey on Lover's Lass, one of western Canada's leading riders. Lover's Lass just scampers outa the gate on top, hangs on the wood as they say, just goes round the track like a hoop round a barrel. Pays the limit . . . better'n twenty to one. Old Copper's feeling pretty good, O geez, he's feeling like Diamond Jim Brady.

Cooper heads back to his hotel, goes up to the desk, asks for the key to his room. Fellow hands him the key, says, "Here's your key, Mr. Cooper." Just something about the way he says "Mr. Cooper" makes Ralph wonder, "Geez, I wonder who *that* was addressed to? Don't think it was for my benefit." Heads over to the elevator bank and, by gosh, sure as hell, sure as god made little green apples, there's another fellow in step with him. Gets on to the elevator, rides up to his floor. Elevator stops, he gets out, the other fellow gets out. Heads down the hall, the other fellow's right on his heels. Just as he's touching the lock on his door, the door opens and there's a fellow in the room says, "Come on in. I'd like to make your acquaintance." Fellow behind him, now right on his arse; he's got no choice. Goes right in there, there's about fifteen fellows in his room, place is fulla smoke, smells of whiskey, some of them sitting on the bed playing cards, others just having a cigar.

Guy takes over, says, "Mr. Cooper, you're from Saskatchewan?" Pronounces it kinda funny like Sas*KAT*chewan. "That's right," Cooper says.

"That was your horse that win today?" guy asks, "Lover's Lass?"

"That's right," Cooper says again.

"You can prove that's Lover's Lass?"

"That's right," again.

"How can you do that?"

"I had her fired in the winter by Doc So-and-So," Cooper says, "Doc So-and-So out in California."

"That so? Can you get hold of him?"

"Yes, I can," Cooper says, "I think maybe I can."

"Well, you better do it. Cause if you wanna go out of this room alive, by the door you come in, instead of outa the window, you better convince us that's Lover's Lass. We ain't had a legitimate caper like that since Man o'War."

So Cooper phones out to the coast, gets hold of the vet . . . he's lucky he does . . . and they pay the vet's way to fly from Los Angeles right to Chicago. They tell the vet if he can get out to Sportsman's Park in the morning, and identify that mare as Lover's Lass, the one he operated on in the winter in Los Angeles, everything's okay.

In the meantime, Cooper's a prisoner in the room with all them guys sitting there. They order food, booze, whatnot in, they just sit there. Cooper's got an awful lot of money coming to him if this works out. His mind's going like a triphammer, he don't know what to think. By geez, the phone rings, head man answers the phone and he says,

"Yeah . . . uh huh . . . yep . . . okay then, that's all I wanted to know." Hangs up.

"Mr. Cooper, we owe you a lotta money. Congratulations. Now, we're gonna tell you a few things. When you get your money, go home to Canada and don't ever bring a sonofabitch of a horse like that down here again. That's one. The other is, if you wanna pass any action our way on football games or whatever the hell they do up there, we'll be delighted to back you up."

So there *is* some honor among thieves, you know . . . some thieves anyways.

Lover's Lass . . . I seen her run at the old Dufferin Park right here in Toronto. Hell of a mare . . . geez she run good. Boys, could she ever rattle outa that gate and get over there on that rail . . . the jock'd be leaning right over the rail as she come round, you'd figure she'd take the skin right off her shoulders.

In Toronto they had what they used to call the "leaky-roof circuit." The old Incorporated Canadian Racing Association, the ICRA. It was a federation of track owners that controlled the racing at the seven thoroughbred tracks in Ontario. In the city of Toronto itself there was Dufferin Park, a half miler, Thorncliffe and Woodbine, a couple of mile tracks. Then, out in Long Branch, just outside the city, there was the track called Long Branch. Then over at Hamilton they had Hamilton, and at Fort Erie, Fort Erie, and at Stamford, Stamford. Them seven tracks made up the old leaky-roof circuit until E.P. Taylor come along, and got control of them all, and revolutionized everything by closing most of them down, renovating what few he had left – the old Woodbine and Fort Erie – and then building a brand new one at Woodbine out by the airport which opened in 1956.

Dufferin and Long Branch was two of the tracks the old horseplayers remember the most for the reason that them was the tracks you had the most fun at. Old Fred Orpen . . . he owned the pair of them . . . he was a terrific promoter. He'd stand in the doorway and give envelopes away that held what he called "daily passes" . . . he hadda deck of passes just like theatre or hockey tickets. You'd get an envelope, they had fourteen days of racing, there'd be fourteen tickets in that envelope, and all you'd have to do is pay a service charge of a few pennies at your way in the door, and that was the tax on the admission. You really felt you were a big timer with this envelope, and I think practically every horseplayer in the city of Toronto had them passes in the envelope. But, you know, you'd go through a big routine of taking them out at the door and coming in. That way he kinda made everyone feel they was members of something, you get the idea.

Geez, the old train used to go out to the Long Branch track and sit on the siding there. I mind the time when old Fred Orpen would stand down at the gate of his Dufferin Park track on Dufferin Street, just south of the Alka-Seltzer plant . . . that used to be a code with Boomer. Always get around Winnie or Nellie Parsons, another old ball-and-chain of mine in the old days, by saying to Boomer, "I'll meet you at the Alka-Seltzer plant," and they'd say, "What's that all about?" And I'd say, "Well, Boomer works in the seltzer division." That was the code for going to Dufferin Park.

Orpen'd stand by the main gate, geez, you'd see women roll up there . . . O boys, with their army boots laced up to their hips, hotter'n a firecracker, their bloomers in a real knot, saying, "Was my old man in the track last night on pay day?" And Orpen'd say,

"Well, I don't know who your old man is, how would I know that?" And, of course, he'd be absolutely right. Geez, she'd flash a picture of him, maybe a wedding picture . . . lotta them come right down with any old thing they could lay their hands on, and she'd say,

"Did you ever see this fellow here?" And Orpen'd say,

"Well, I never did see him but if I ever do again he won't be allowed in. What happened?" Well, she'd say,

"He come in here with his Toronto Transportation Commission cheque and blew the whole dang thing."

"Well," Orpen'd say, "How much was that?" The woman'd say,

"Well, it was $33.76 . . ." or whatever it was in them days and he'd reach into his pocket, get the money out, and then he'd have one of his fellows drive the woman home. He'd tell the boys, "See this picture of this fellow? Tell the gatemen I don't ever want to find this guy inside the grounds." Orpen had a damned good photographic memory, if he seen a guy he'd say, "Out!"

Orpen cared about his people, you know, he'd take the old lemon pie home from the track restaurant and put it right on the dining room table. Figured if it was good enough for his horseplayers, his patrons, it was good enough for his family . . . or the other way around.

I think that the thing Orpen's remembered for most is the fact that he thought he was some kinda piano player. You know, they often say if so-and-so had to sing for shit they wouldn't get a smell. There's no way in the world he was ever gonna give Paderewski a run for his money . . . or Liberace either . . . you get the idea. He had a repertoire that, to say the least, was limited. He knew "Auld Lang Syne," the national anthem . . . that's "God Save the King" in them days . . . He could do "Goodnight Irene" . . . he had a daughter name of Irene, lovely looking girl. He did "Don't Sit Under the Apple Tree" . . . That seemed to be a message to the horseplayers, you know, between races all of a sudden you'd hear this piano serenade. Well, there was no apple tree on the property but somehow it was if the old man was telling you something . . . "Don't Sit Under the Apple Tree" . . . don't sit on your hands, get up and bet your money, sorta thing.

Orpen had a terrific announcer at his tracks, guy name of Foster Buck Dryden . . . that was his real name. He was an old racetracker, owned a few horses of his own, had a horse name of Hard Facts. Buck, aside from liking the women and the horses, liked his juice once in a while, you know, used to get into the sauce, not too often. By the enda the season, after the old wheel had ground just about to a halt, he'd be kinda stepping himself up a few lengths by reaching for the bottle before he went on the public address system for the first race. I mind one time poor old Buck was really in his cups, and he was calling all the horses that was in the next race for the first race on the card. He had his program open to the second race when it was the first race that was on.

Geez, everyone in the place was laughing, everyone was looking at their program, looking up at him, he was up there, large as life, standing all alone on the roof, he had a kinda little booth. It was a funny place, Dufferin Park; you could get into the infield, between races you could cross the track on a kinda duckboard. Well geez, the public address system's still on. All of a sudden, everyone in the joint hears this voice . . . O, it's Fred Orpen sure as hell . . . saying,

"Buck?" Then we hear . . . this is Buck's voice,

"Yes, Mr. Orpen."

"Buck, you called the wrong horses in that race."

"Yes, Mr. Orpen."

"Buck, you'd better call the right horses in the next race."

"Yes, Mr. Orpen."

"Buck, you better pull up your socks."

"Yes, Mr. Orpen."

Well, the next race comes on now, the race Buck has already called comes up. By geez, it's a funny thing. The real race features the same horses Buck had called in error. Geez, that Buck sure knew his horseflesh. Same dang horses go out one-two that went out in his imaginary call . . . I can still remember, they was Mountain Lion and . . . and . . . I forget the other. They run one-two all the way round. That was about all he could do, he just spot them two, the rest in the pack he never sorted out at all.

Geez, after awhile we hear on the loudspeakers,

"Buck?"

"Yes, Mr. Orpen."

"That was much better."

"Thank you, Mr. Orpen."

I remember one day at Dufferin a Frenchman who had some horses, fellow name of Andy Pion from Quebec. Orpen had some dang promotion where he had a gold shovel and he made Pion, who was leading trainer at the meet, dig a hole right by the winner's circle and dig up a sack of silver dollars or something he buried there . . . Orpen was always doing some dang fool thing like that. Orpen was on the microphone, describing this silly event and all through his spiel he must've said the name "Pion" twenty times. Finally, some old hack comes outa the crowd and shouts, "Pion Orpen" and that brought the house down.

Poor old Buck Dryden was really tested whenever a mare name of York Hunt showed up on the entries. I guess a little bit of history's in order here. Toronto's original name at one time used to be York, named after one of the king's sons. Citizens later got together, held a vote, changed the name from York to Toronto. But there was a hunt club started at that time, named after the king's son. Come to think of it, it might have been a name chosen by a real wiseacre cause York Hunt is one hell of a name to say.

By geez, Buck was an awful prim and proper sonofagun and

he'd just never call that mare by her given name. I mind one time out at the old Long Branch, and York Hunt made a tremendous move outa the pack, and really started to threaten coming to the quarter pole. Geez, Buck was calling a couple horses in front of the mare and then he says, " . . . you-know-her-name's running third on the outside." Then, when the field turned for home, by geez, he names the leader and the horse in the second spot and " . . . you-know-who flying on the outside." Then, by the time they're hitting the sixteenth pole, old Buck's now saying, " . . . and you-know-her-name now going to the front." Every guy in the lunch-pail gang would just do his damndest, if he had his money down on her, to be shouting, "Come on, York Hunt! come on, York Hunt!"

I remember one time, by geez, it was the off season, a couple of months before the bugle was to sound for the first race. You know what they say about the idle mind being the devil's workshop . . . there I was around the house, Boomer and Winnie kinda stall-walking with me. By geez, we jumped into Boomer's old Terraplane, and before you could say Jack Robinson, there we was sitting in the parking lot at the Woodbine, cranking the windows down and pretending we could hear Darryl Wells calling the races. Now that's pretty desperate.

I remember they held a race meet in White Rock, British Columbia, by geez the favorites swept the card. Next week they held a meet and the favorites swept the card again. And do you know that meet went absolutely stone bonkers broke for the reason that no one is interested in running down to White Rock and backing a favorite, and cashing a two-buck ticket and getting two-ten back.

Austin Taylor, who has been mentioned before, is a fellow who made a fortune in mining in British Columbia . . . matter of fact, he owned some pretty fair horses in his time. He owned Indian Broom who was third in the Kentucky Derby in 1936. Taylor was British Columbia's biggest owner, and in his day he was the first Canadian to have a horse finish in the money in the derby since old Commodore J.K.L. Ross of Montreal had Sir Barton in 1919.

Geez, one day Taylor bet on one of his horses at Lansdowne. He had all these fifty-buck win tickets. He figures he was going to get five cents on the two dollars, geez he must've bought a fistful of fifty buckers. He goes to cash his tickets and all he gets is a nickle on each fifty-dollar ticket. He never knew that in the fine print of the rules of racing for the province of British Columbia the sneaky track operators changed from "a nickle minimum payoff on a two-dollar ticket" to "a minimum nickle payoff on *a* ticket." O, was he hot, he jumped up and down on his hat in fronta the grandstand. Hotter'n a firecracker. That made all the old winos and regulars just laugh their heads off. They thought, "By god, here's a multi-millionaire and the bastards have got to him."   ●

9
Not Much Canadian Broadcasting, but One Hell of a Lotta Corporation

I guess you could talk till the cows come home on things that's a real no-no. I mind the time I was working for the American Can Company. In them days the American Can Company in Vancouver had been organized by the CIO steelworkers. That's in the days when Canada, in the labor movement, we had both the CIO and the AF of L, at least in English-speaking Canada. Before the Canadian Labor Congress. Both CIO and the AFL was big American international unions, and they had the money and the organization knowhow to come up and organize the workers in Canada. Wherever you look you could say the thirties in Canada was when the automobile boys was organized in Oshawa, Ontario – much to the chagrin of Mitch Hepburn, the premier in them days.

Well, out in Vancouver, we had the CIO steelworkers in American Can and every so often a union in Vancouver by the name of the Boomnet Tendermen (or else an association, I'm not sure it was a union,) would go out on strike just at the time of the herring catch. By geez, the CIO steelworkers at American Can would go out in sympathy. There we'd be with a sign standing out in fronta the can plant. Insteada inside making the herring cans for the herring catch, we'd be outside on strike. What do you think was happening? Here's an international union story that I've mentioned right at District 6 steelworkers' meeting at the Mount Royal Hotel in Montreal. And you could hear a pin drop when I laid it on them. But geez, a lot of the fellows come up to me after and says, "Freddy boy, I wanna thank you for having the guts to lay that one on us, we needed to hear it." So here we was, back in the good old days of the CIO steelworkers union, in Vancouver, out on a sympathy strike with the Boomnet Tenders. And the American Can Company was closed right down – Canco they called it.

What do you think happens? The Brotherhood of Railway Workers hauls cans made in the American Can Company plant in Seattle, over the border, right slick and clean past our plant in Vancouver down to the docks. So as soon as we was out on sympathy strike with the Boomnet Tendermen, our brother workers was benefiting in the nearest place to us, Seattle, Washington, to the tune of extra shifts put on to pick up the slack. Every so often in the *Vancouver Sun* and the *Province*, you'd see that 40,000 woodworkers or 60,000 woodworkers are out on strike in BC; it's the goddamndest place for people going on strike. What do you think happens? The mills in Washington and Oregon immediately double up their shifts – there's overtime and double time and god knows what. And their brother workers is just benefiting to the tune of screwing the poor s.o.b.s up in Vancouver like you wouldn't know what.

Most strikes in BC is broken by the housewives. They get sick, sore, and tired of the old man hanging around the house with nothing to do. They finally send the bastard back to work. That's how the strikes is broken, not broke by the bosses any more – they're broke by the women. As a matter of fact I seen a movement one time where them women was all banded together saying they was going to hold out on their menfolk – they wouldn't give them *nothing* unless they went back to work. Can you imagine that? And that happened before International Women's Year.

I've always remembered what old Elmore Philpott . . . what a wonderful WASP name, Philpott. The Celts and the WASPS have the *nerve* to laugh at anyone else with a so-called funny, foreign name. By geez, Philpott! . . . Anyways, old Elmore Philpott, wonderful old windbag, used to write a syndicated column at the time of World War II. And he wrote one time, I'll *never* forget, "Until the Canadian labor movement divorces itself from the international union movement of North America, strikes out on its own as an independent outfit, answerable only to itself, will the trade union movement in Canada ever take a big step forward."

There's an awful lot of people in the union movement in Canada – professional union boys – who should have been selling brassieres or corsets in Marks and Spencer. Instead they're over here in big union jobs telling our fellows how to do things. Just because they can talk a little better, that's because they had a better education.

Anyways, you'd never read in the paper in Vancouver what a wicked situation that was with the boys from American Can out on strike supporting the Boomnet Tendermen and their brother workers, same union, working at the same plant in Seattle screwing them right to the wall. You'd wait till hell froze over before you read that. *That's* the kinda stuff that oughta be in the paper, that's a story – that's getting down to the nub of it. Talk about multinational corporations. Put some of the international unions in the same category. Screwing this country, that's the best way to look at it. That's the first and foremost way to look at it. They claim, because they're international unions, they've gotta act this way, because they can't cut the mustard any other way. I say bullshit – too much of their money goes out of the country and it ain't a two-way street. When our boys are out looking up Toby's arse, they're cashing in on it. And when they're out, we're following right in line and we're out too. So what's good for the goose is *not* good for the gander.

A reporter goes out on a story and he finds out that a hell of a lot

of new Ford owners is sick and tired of the cars they bought
rusting. Right through the fenders in no time at all. Right from the
time they listened to the final gasp of bullshit from the order-taker
who sold them the bloody car in the first place, until six months of
rusting. All that rusting. By geez, what do you think happens? The
Ford rust owners have to get together and form an association to
get some kinda redress, cause the company's gotta policy. This has
been in the press, and if the press means anything since it costs
fifteen cents, it must mean you *can* buy the truth for that, wouldn't
you think? I mean if they print it, it must be right.

Have we ever got the most sweetheart set-up with libel laws in
this country. Every damn shyster has hid behind them for years. It
don't matter what you're doing, by the time you got the goods on
someone, the lawyers who look it over – whether it's TV or radio or
the press – they'll say "O you can't do this, or you can't say that,
we could be in court."

Did you ever try going to court in this country? A friend of mine
sued somebody, sued them for breach of contract and damages.
Two years, eight months later he finally got to court. Spent two
and a half days there trying to prove his case. Then you know what
happened? The judge says, "I'll let you know." You know what the
system's designed for? It's designed for the people you're suing to
get together with you to figure it out so you don't end up in court.
In other words, fellow, forget it. Unless you got the time *and the
money,* you might as well look up a dead horse's arse.

Geez, the Granville Street bridge in Vancouver was a wonderful
boondoggle for a lotta us, you know. I hired on as a rod man. I was
up passing the time of day with another fellow. Geez, all of a
sudden the foreman says, "Dobbs, come on over here," I says,
"Yeah?" and I doubled over to where he was. I remember there
was a hot, blazing sun that day, not the usual kind of dirty-shirt
Vancouver sky you get most of the time. He says, "You told me
you was a rod man back east." I says "That's right." "Well" he
says, "You sure as hell ain't one out west." So that was the end of
that one. Most of the people I knew got hired on the Granville
Street bridge and I like to think I spent a bit of the time of day on
it myself. She was a big eight-laner. A lotta people say to me,

what's a rod man. I still to this day don't know.

Did you ever meet anyone who didn't have to lie for a job in this country? Unless you graduated with a PhD in leather work or something, then you went down to a tannery and they'd hire you on as a historian or something. Most of us have had to tell some fantastic big Toby about how experienced we is. Until this day, I couldn't tell you what a rod man is. But I got four hours pay anyway, which was enough to get me on the old interurban and out to Lansdowne and I think I fell on my arse after the double. So that was the end of that act.

The media accounts to no one but its owners, when you get right down to it. The real tragedy of course is – we're harrowing up the same old ground – it's the censorship of the people in the game that's imposed on the proceedings of things by themselves. It's like when "This Hour Has Seven Days" was a big hit on TV in Canada. All the academics in the country got into a flap cause it didn't have Professor Dulldrawers on beating his gums about the theory of something – it had *real* people and challenges. It was designed in such a way as to create a lotta confrontations. In effect, it had all the magic of showbiz and Sunday night and it was a real kinda thing for everyone to sit down and watch. It was the first public affairs show in Canada that the man in the street actually watched. He didn't feel he was going to get Einstein's theory of relativity, and some assistant to the prime minister talking for three hours on the Mackenzie King papers of 1927. Or how to set an oboe score for an Allan King documentary on a fire hydrant up in Baffinland. Here you had a show that appealed to more than a million people, that dealt with the things that was going on in the country.

Now they took a lotta cheap shots. They had poor old Horsburg, the minister that was peeking at kids going at it, and that wasn't hitting at anyone who had any power. As far as I'm concerned, if you're gonna do a real show you hit the guys that have got power. So now you're up against someone who cuts the mustard, do you get the idea, instead of some poor old guy in a clerical collar.

Anyway, in the main, the show was exciting and it had the right idea. But ever since then, the lid's been on. The mandate has been: We don't wanna whole lot of requests for transcripts, and a whole lotta requests for screenings every Monday morning after the show. We wanna have a little peace. We wanna be able to come in at ten o'clock, have a one-hour meeting, go for a three-hour liquid lunch, and catch the GO train at four. Cause that's the way it should be. You know what I mean? Don't it just rot your socks?

And the way we clown around and tailgate every United States story. The way we revel in their misery – that's a real cheap shot on the part of the *Toronto Globe and Mail*. Geez, I remember old Tommy Douglas in the House of Commons, waving a fistful of clippings from the *Globe*. That would lend currency to something he had to say, so long as he had the clipping in his mitt. The *Globe* spends half of its time telling us about what a dreadful place the US of A is. Well, that's all right. I guess anywhere you go in the world, if you're ten percent of the population of your neighbor and they own you, they've got you right by the bag. I guess you can whine and puke away about how mean they is. But, I think there's a lotta hypocrisy to it.

This brings to mind the whole "ring-around-the-rosie" circle jerk situation you got in the east of Canada right now – I'm saying the "east of Canada" not for the reason I want to get everyone's shorts in a knot in British Columbia, or the prairies, or Quebec or the Maritimes – I'm saying it for the reason that we're dealing with about a third of the country's population, and it wouldn't matter to me if they was all living at Mahone Bay or south of Wetaskiwin. The fact is, we're talking about seven and a half to eight million people, and the kinda media molly-hoxing they put up with, and the rest of the country gets the spillover. I'm talking about the circle jerk of the CBC, the *Toronto Star*, *Maclean's* magazine. Right now, in the golden age of bullshit, we got Peter Newman, editor of *Maclean's* magazine, author of the bestseller, *The Establishment*. Here's a guy who's gone to every club in Canada, once, and done a rundown on the country's upper 400. Lottsa good stories. I gotta kick out of the one about Bud McDougald, the chairman of the board of Argus Corporation, walking along with Bobby Kennedy saying, "I'll put up a million bucks for every million you'll put up for charity." Bobby Kennedy never come up with a penny. Newman let the air out of the rubbers of a lotta people – didn't spice it up with much bedroom stuff. Anyway, here's Peter Newman selling his book *The Establishment* to the CBC who're gonna come out with a real ballbreaker on all these drearies. A big prime-time sleeporama.

The worst thing that ever happened to Canada was when old John Bassett threw the towel in and sold the *Toronto Telegram* to the *Toronto Star*. That was the absolute living end for competition for the big evening newspapers in the province of Ontario. Now don't you provincial s.o.b.s rise up off your honkers and start yapping about Toronto with a capital *T*.

We'll get right into that one and tear the mask off once and for all.

Take the CBC, they've got the country divided into five regions. For the English language, all the biggies have to work in the city of Toronto. If there's one thing they love beating their gums about in the regions, it's the sonsofbitches in Toronto, dumping on the regions. But, the one thing they don't know in the regions is, the sonsofbitches in Toronto all *come* from the regions. Anyone that ever cut the mustard in broadcasting in Canada, left the regions around the time of Marconi. In other words, if you're in Vancouver, Calgary, Edmonton, Winnipeg, Fredericton, St. John's or whatever, and you're being dumped on by someone from Toronto, you're being dumped on by someone who was born, raised, and worked in Halifax, Winnipeg, or Vancouver.

The fact that he's passing through Toronto is something else again. There hasn't been a Toronto man make a big decision in broadcasting since Lorne Greene invented god. But it suits the regional small-time thinking of all these places to yammer about that particular fact. They've never got it straight, but I'm getting it straight in this here book right now. Name me all the people who run the CBC and I'll put the correct labels on them – Vancouver, Calgary, Edmonton, Winnipeg, Halifax, but you won't find Toronto. You might find some pipsqueak town somewhere in Ontario that's generated some fellow who's made a minor impression in chamber music on FM radio, or CBC farms or some other big ballbreaker. But the people who cut the mustard in the corporation has all come from the cities and towns in the regions.

All this explains why the CBC is such a grubby, little, provincial organization. Because the people who run it have never gotten over the rotten little tiny-mind ideas they had in the first place. There's not a cosmopolitan mind, there's not a man who can carry on a sophisticated conversation. There's not anyone who can laugh at the whole world of UBC, U of Man, Western U, or Dalhousie and do it with aplomb. No sir, they take them degrees real serious, that's why they nail them on the wall along with their RCAF pilot officers' certificates. They actually nail them on the wall, for god's sakes.

You can forgive a dentist for putting his diplomas up cause his old lady probably come down to his office and says, "Put this thing up on the wall, so people will know where you learned what you know." You go to the CBC for an expert and you'll find some fellow who's either on the faculty of a university or he's working for a newspaper. He's running in and out of the CBC picking up pocket money because the CBC doesn't give a damn about developing broadcasters. All they wanna do is keep anyone who might rise up against them quiet. That's why when they go to something like the Olympics, or when they cover political conventions, they don't have enough broadcasters to really do anything. They'll cry "unfair," because they have the Liberal Party chip-on-the-shoulder, hide-behind-the-desk attitude when anyone levels a criticism at them. Their whole *raison d'etre* (I picked that one up because I wanna be a little bilingual once in awhile) is to shout "unfair." Bullshit – that's exactly the way it is.

These ostrich-in-the-sand, anti-intellectuals, full-time bureaucratic dummies have their hands on the balls of the media of this country. It's absolutely frightening. If you summoned the heads of news and public affairs for all of television and radio into one room, you'd see that very few of them's got any courage. Very few of them's got any real integrity, and very few of them is really newsmen. They sure are the people to have in them sensitive positions, because they're forever gonna go by the old credo: "If it's not in the *Globe and Mail*, or *Free Press*, or the *Vancouver Sun*, it can't be true." Isn't that perfect?

What the dumb reporter can't stop, Beland Honderich or some

other powerful publisher *will* stop. Speaking of Honderich of the *Toronto Star*, hundreds of pages, especially in their Saturday edition, for thirty-five cents, closest thing you'll get to the *New York Times* as far as size and weight goes, furthest as far as anything else goes. Course unless you're reading the houses-for-sale, or the cars-for-sale want ads, you can skim through the whole gutless thing in about twelve minutes flat. Take it out to your outhouse, but don't reach for it if you run out of paper. The print on it will come off on your hand and your arse and that's not a good situation to be in.

What really gives me a laugh is the editorial page feature on a Saturday, where they trot out old Borden Spears to beat his gums on the things that he figures just wasn't copasetic in the last week. This is kinda like the Manitoba dentists policing the Dental Act of Manitoba, or the Canadian Police Chief's Association having the divine right to investigate the suicides of police chiefs across Canada.

By the way, if anybody ever wants to do a study or a history on a phenomenon in the Canadian way of life . . . which, incidentally, would be a real breakthrough in the age of bullshit . . . they should take it upon themselves to maybe suck up to some of them *literati* of Canada and get a Canada Council grant and do a study on why so many police chiefs of Canadian cities, towns, and villages has bumped themselves off since the year 1900. Now, what do you think of that for a Freddy Dobbs outburst! Does that let the air outa your rubbers, cause if it don't, it should.

Yessiree, there's been dozens of men in this century who was chief constables of villages, towns, and cities and they bumped themselves off. Sure, the golden age of B.S.'s been around for quite a while, hasn't it? Course, we're in the absolute *golden* age in the seventies. But I'll bet you never knew that one. That's an interesting one, ain't it? How would Canadians know it when they're watching foolish old Jack Webb, and "The FBI Story" and "Kojak"? Is there any way they're gonna know it watching all that junk? No way in the world. Incidentally, that explains why when someone comes to your door and knocks on it, or rings your bell, you open it. Don't you remember? For years Jack Webb'd be there, he'd say, "Ma'am," flash his badge and he'd be in. Sonofabitch could've unzipped himself and he'd still be in.

By geez, it's a funny thing when you think about Canada; you got Lord Thomson of Fleet, he had more newspapers than Lake Erie's got polluted fish and probably, in this day and age, was as powerful as Lord Northcliffe was around the time of World War I in Britain. Course, Max Bell's gone now, that's *FP Publications*, the *Globe and Mail*, *Vancouver Sun* the *Ottawa Journal*, *Lethbridge Herald*, the *Albertan* in Calgary, *Winnipeg Free Press* and, O geez, lots more.

But when all's said and done, the old Atkinson Charitable Foundation, was meant to prevent the *Toronto Star* from being annihilated by the Ontario government. The nemesis of the *Star* has always been the Ontari-ari-ari-ario Tory government. The old Atkinson Charitable Foundation was set up so's the *Star* could carry on with its wondrous works of being all things to all people.

We'll be talking to you. ●

10
"You're British and Don't You Ever Forget It!"

It's a funny thing: here we is past the old quarter pole of the twentieth century with three quarters of the nineteen hundreds showing her heels to us like some nineteenth-century European kingdom, and we're still trying to discover nationalism. Geez, I thought nationalism went out with the dodo bird except for them brand new emerging African states like Chad or Bomboland or maybe Israel – but Canada? Kinda makes you stop and think when you realize we were past the old century mark in 1967, don't it?

I can remember my old school principal getting blood red in the face because he said some dirty Canadianism was rearing its head in the classroom. O geez, I can remember it real good. He was a minister, canon in the church of England and could he ever fire a salvo when he wanted to, but he sure was a funny man of the cloth. Always used to have on a shiny black suit. He had a kinda perverted way of straddling the students; he'd have you lean over, you know, and touch your toes sitting at your desk, and then the sonofabitch would sit on you like you was a damn human bicycle seat. His neck, when he would get hot, would turn blood red, and it would just bulge out of one of them tight clerical collars, you know. Once in a while we'd get a real good look at them and he'd have a paper clip holding the whole thing together. He looked like his head was a big tomato, and that was when he was red with rage all because someone in our classroom dared to stand up, and maybe demonstrate a bitta pride they'd got from their home. You never know where it all comes from. How do you know where kids get what it is they're gonna say, how do you know?

The other day I seen a kid running down the street shouting, "I found a prophylatic, I found a prophylatic, I found a prophylatic on the verandah." Sorta singsong. Another kid runs across and say, "What's a verandah?" I mean, you don't know nowadays. It's like when Winnie was answering the door around the time of Halloween, a little kid's standing there just as cute as a bug's ear. Couldn't have been any more than six years of age, all decked out like a pirate. Winnie goes right along with it. She bought, god love her old gold heart, she went out and bought all kinda things to give away. She said, "Geez, ain't you cute? You're all dressed up like a little pirate," and he nods and says, "Trick or treat." Then Winnie says, "Where's your buccaneers?" He looks right up at Winnie, bold as brass, don't skip a beat, and says, "Under my buccan hat."

But there we was, sitting in the classroom, and some kid said something about being Canadian. O geez, already the old principal's eyes is shooting fire, insteada walking calm, he's stomping up and down. He'd always have a sorta dickie outfit, the church calls it, his dickie tucked into his jeans. Couldn't help thinking how funny he looked, kinda all covered over in a kind of bluey haze except for his arms. His head had an awful jaw, always set in a real mean way – he hated kids, you could tell that. Somehow his style of going on shattered any ideas I might ever have of god's men moving in a hysterious and kinda dignified way.

Anyways, there he was – blowing a gasket – shouting and roaring, "You're British and don't you ever forget it! You're British, fellow, you're British, and don't you ever forget it!" Funny thing, but when he'd come to rest and he was all done, he'd be standing under the picture we had there of the king, one of the Georges – one with a beard. Bright red tunic on, lotsa medals, and a sorta crimson sash, silver and gold things. The class goodygoodies, of course, would always sing out "God Save the King" real loud, and insteada standing at attention, the way a soldier does, they'd freeze up in some awkward-looking, real, stiff stance staying with it until they'd shouted out the whole thing. The old principal would sorta close his eyes and rock back on his heels and make like he was communicating with the king, or maybe it was supposed to be god *and* the king, it was hard to know, but either way, he give the impression he was right there with them giving them the time of day.

I could always see the old principal there, used to picture him in his red shorts, leading the whole darn shooting match. Right there in my mind's eye, I could see hundreds of old school principals, all done up in red, white, and blue, their white collars so tight, their big, fat, red heads redder than red, all shouting, "You're British, and don't you forget it!" By geez, they'd say it over and over again, trapping the guilty ones into the ground. I can see him running all round the classroom, never mind riding on the shoulder blades, rocking back and forth, getting his thrills.

Geez, enough about my old principal; funny how things that happen when you're a kid remain so clear in the old memory. Let's talk about the way things is today.

When you're in the working force you don't blow into work at 9:30, and get a three-hour liquid lunch, and then screw off at 4:00. It's a funny thing, the fellows who come home all gassed up, and ride the elevators back to their offices, and lament the little advances the postal workers or whatever make, they're always on the three-hour liquid lunch, have you ever noticed, that's their credentials. Fair is fair, eh? No it ain't, it is not.

It's kinda like old Tarzan blowing home around about five in the evening, shocking the hell outa Jane. By geez, she comes in and says, "What are you doing home?" "Jane," he says, "I want a martini." She says, "Okay," and gets him a martini. By geez, he knocks it back real quick and then asks her for a double. She says, "Tarzan, you never have more than one martini, what's got inta you?" He says, "Jane, it's a jungle out there.

You know, back in the old days you'd make twenty cents a day working on an airfield or something at Penfield Ridge, New Brunswick. By geez, we used to bunk right on the old landing strip and then go into Saint John on the weekend. Supposed to be a training base but they never did use it on accounta the fog. Wicked altogether, but that was the god's honest truth. Back in them days there was more meal hours than there was meals.

Worked right alongside fellows who told me about the days when their fathers, up in the bush, would harness them up, just like you'd harness up a work horse, to clear the land of rocks. One friend of mine lost all his brothers and sisters, they all died of consumption, they all was in harness at one time or another. It's an awful life for some people, you know. The only thing for sure seems to be death and taxes. Them days we used to head for some place where you could really wet your whistle. But I tell you, with the wages they was paying, you could only tie one on the one night, then it was a case of kinda laying in until it was time to get back to the base. We all knew about the fog, but no one beat their gums too much about it. It was something no one ever mentioned. Britain was talking up a plan for training her boys, so as they could fly something they called the British Empire Training Scheme.

Old Mackenzie King, always keeping his ear to the ground on where the next vote was coming from, put the kibosh on that one. King even went further than that, he even called up old Hitler. Can you imagine that? Maybe King got the message in one of them seances we all keep hearing about, maybe King knew about the fog at Penfield Ridge. If you're ever down in the Maritimes some day you can still see the runway we built, and, you know, often times nowadays Air Poland ain't running into Saint John and you know why – it's because of the fog.

Met a fellow from Prague, Czechoslovakia, he got out when the Germans come along, just got out by the skin of his teeth. Note I says "Germans," not Nazis, that's because I like to call a spade a spade. Ever since World War II, there's been another kinda bullshit all to do with "be kind to Germany." It's a wonder they don't have tag days. You take the war in Vietnam, we've just had that one. Now, no one ever talked about the Democrats and the Republicans from the United States fighting the Viet Cong. No, they talked about the United States army, you get the idea. So, when the Germans did the Czechs in, this fellow managed to get out because a friend of his, well there's no other way of putting it, he was a real pro-German type and they was friends, so he tipped him off. There was something wrong with him, according to the Germans and according to a lotta Czechs who liked Germans, trouble was he was Jewish. So, he was tipped off not to go home on this certain day cause he was told they'd be looking for him. Now, can you imagine being in your late teenage years coming home from school, and all of a sudden one of your best friends comes up to you and tells you to scram?

Now, the two of you has never had no discussion about politics or nothing like that, but your best friend's in the know about something and you *know* he is just cause of the way he's talking to you, and the way he's looking at you. He says don't go home, they're looking for you. When translated, what he's saying is, "The people that I think is wonderful, that's walked into our country, don't happen to like the likes of you, so they're looking for you." But, he was making an exception – you're a friend of mine. That was more important. Kinda funny, eh?

Well he didn't go home. Geez, this friend of his even fixed him up with fake identification papers, and everything, and he went right down to the train, and had a lot of real rough times crossing one border after another. But, he got all the way to England, and never again seen his friend who gave him all the papers, and tipped him off, never seen his mother again, and father, and brothers, and sisters who was back home there. His dad worked at night. Germans come and took them all away and that was the last anyone ever heard of them. His friend joined the German army, and like millions of others, he never come home from the war, either. No one's ever heard of him. You never know, though, he may be working as a dishwasher in Winnipeg or a logger in British Columbia, if he's lucky.

I'm going all round Cape Horn here, because I'm talking about my old Czechoslovakian friend, Otto, who joined up in England with the Czech air force. He told me, he said, you know, "It's a funny thing Fred, you're talking about what does Canada mean to you. Can you imagine the kinda shock I got when I run into Canadians, for the first time in my life, in the air force, and I was at a Canadian air force base, and there was all these fellows over from Canada, dressed up in their air force uniforms, and you know what they're doing? They're hanging Mackenzie King in effigy in their mess, laughing their heads off, getting drunker than farts. That was my introduction to Canada and the people from Canada who had come to England to try and help win the war."

He says they done it not once, but they done it many, many times. He never got over that and he always used to laugh when he'd tell that, his eyes would light up and he had wonderful even teeth, and to him that was just the most wonderful thing that people could be fighting on one side against another, fighting for a cause or whatever it was, but nevertheless string their leader up in effigy. He said, by geez, he sure knew he was with a different outfit than the ones he had run away from. He sure knew that. There was no way anyone would hang old Reichmarshall Göering in effigy – they might have wanted to but they never had the balls to, they never had the freedom to. That's for goddamn sure. So that's something about being Canadian in a roundabout way.

You know, old Mackenzie King showed up as the head of Canada to review a lotta Canadian troops one time in England. Geez, it was raining cats and dogs, and King kept them standing in the rain for three hours. When he finally showed up, by geez, they all got together and gave him the raspberry. O geez, was he ever hotter'n a firecracker about that! Can you imagine a buncha limey soldiers lining up and booing Churchill? Or let's go better than that – how about a buncha Germans on parade in Berlin, booing Hitler when he showed up. That's pretty tough to put together, ain't it? Holy doodle, wonder what Mackenzie King's medium said to him on that score when he finally confessed.

What a funny fellow King musta been, eh? Now we know he used to enter in his diary that he went out looking for . . . went

out doing, what do ya call it, a little tom-catting on Jarvis Street
. . . and as soon as he got the job done he'd rush home to his diary
and said, O I never should have done it, never should have done it,
I will never do it again. The sonofabitch'd fold up the diary and be
out on the street again, with a vibration in his knickers. That's the
fellow who ended up leading this country. He wrote all the
sweetheart anti-trust laws, by the way, long ago, that's why it's
practically impossible to get at any of the big fellows nowadays.
We'll get outa the dark ages on that one sometime.

By the way, if you don't know your Canadian paper money too
good, check outa fifty-dollar bill sometime, the new one's kinda
reddish pink color, not the color of the old principal's arse. They're
sorta burgundy I guess. But there's horses' arses on both sides of the
new Canadian fifty-dollar bill. Have a look at one sometime when
you're in a bank. On one side you got the Royal Canadian Mounted
Police musical ride all drawn up in a circle, and it's a real bum
view of them, and on the other side there's a bigger horse's arse
than all the Mounties' horses put together, that's Mackenzie King.
Ain't that something?

Now, I don't mind the Ottawa Liberals helping the mounted
police celebrate their birthday, or whatever. I mean, what better
way than to carry on the best public relations any police force ever
had going for it in the history of man. But Mackenzie King? Geez,
only the nerve of people with the clackers of them that taste power
could immortalize *him!* Now them sentiments is bound to get a
lotta shorts in a knot, especially some Liberal ones.

You see, nothing makes me sick, sore, or tireder than the people
who just sit back in such a comfy way and think everything's
terrific – geez, they're not the people who are glad we've got the
birds, and the bees, and the smell of the trees, and wonderful fresh
fruit, and sorta the feel of love in the air, and so on. No! They're
just sitting back there, fulla their power, they're just the kinda guys
that I sorta see sitting up in the middle of the night and shouting,
"O, that burning itch," when everything goes wrong. It's just like
when you tell a fellow who's all involved with a religion that a man
without god is like a fish without a bicycle. O geez, does that ever
stop him. O geez, he looks at you as if to say, "How dare you say

that?" Well, of course, we can say anything. Why shouldn't we?

Anyways, here I am going all round Cape Horn about my old friend Otto and I'm forgetting the real reason why he came to Canada and stayed here ever since – he married a wonderful Canadian girl. Otto figured it all this way, he says to himself, "This Canada's gotta be alright if her fellows in the air force and soldiers can hang their leader in effigy and then boo him in the flesh when he shows up. It can't be too bad a place." So he figures Canadians must have something in order to permit all that, so he come to Canada and he's never regretted the decision.

I remember one day he was talking – it was in West Vancouver, on of the most beautiful places you'll ever see in the world. By geez, sorta an evergreen mountainside and thousands of people living on the side of the mountain. Old Otto was kinda down, things wasn't going too good his way, and he always got kinda sad, never afraid, kinda man who was never afraid to show his emotions.

He's standing there, and just couldn't shake the thoughts that was torturing him. Getting on in years, he was saying, not young any more, and he should have done this, and he should have done that. How many times have you met a fellow who all of a sudden has decided he has missed the boat? Of course, most of us call it "the change of life" or something. By geez, they'll hook up with anything with a skirt on and make jackfools of themselves, and then they'll come home like whipped dogs and ask forgiveness – most of the time they get it. Kinda funny.

There he was, all down in the dumps, and I couldn't think of nothing to give him, no inspiration, or nothing, and all of a sudden this little boy comes running up the hill towards us, shouting, "Daddy, daddy, you're home, you're home." Geez, I never seen a little face like that, just abeaming and ashining so happy – so fulla love, he was, and just so anxious to show it, and just so fulla the thrill of seeing his dad. I looked at him, and then I looked at old Otto.

"By geez," I said, "I'll tell you something. I might have a lotta independence, and a lotta freedom roaming around from one enda the country to the other, but there's no little face that ever looks to me like that. That's for you, that's your little face, you helped make that, you oughta give yourself a shake. Geez," I says to him, "if you're gonna trudge along through life from here on in, all down at the lip, you maybe just better get down on your prayer handles, and laugh a little, and say, 'Thank god, I still do have the ability to laugh, and the sense to know when someone really cares and loves me.'" He says . . . he wasn't afraid to touch . . . he just slapped me on the back and said, "God friend, you know you're a good man." And, do you know, at that time I actually was a good man. I was just saying something, one man to another, you see, that's the idea.

It's kinda tough to say, what does Canada mean to me? I'm kinda proud of the fact that we allowed our boys to get away with that hanging-in-effigy bullshit. I don't think too many other people did. I've never heard too many people complain about the Canadian air force, World War II, did you? Mind you, not many Canadians nowadays know much about it. How are they gonna when the likes of CTV network puts shows on the air called, what was it, "A History of the Anglo-American Air War Against Germany," and Canada turned up for five seconds in a one-hour show. Wicked altogether, just wicked altogether. No wonder we think that Jack Webb and Kojak's all made in Toronto or Montreal. Little wonder that we think the desert rats, or whoever the hell they was, or the Yanks landed at Dieppe. No wonder we're fulla bullshit when we're fed so much of it.

You know, way back in them days when the Big War, as they used to call it, was on, Canada, when you look back on it, Canada was pretty good – that was when you joined up for king and country – 1914-18, king and country. Now you figure we had only about six millions at that time. An awful lotta people in the land had come from England when all of a sudden everything kinda worked its way to one powerful, awful looking head, which they finally called the August Bank Holiday in 1914. Many of the fellows had just come off the boat, turned right round after joining up and, by geez, they was crossing the pond again.

For a country with only six million people, we done awful good when you consider that from that number – exactly ten percent of our population – 600,000 – were in the uniform of this country, joined up, volunteered, never mind no draft, none of that bullshit, went down, as they said at the time, for king and country. Shows you, though, how people was brainwashed in them days cause when you come forward to 1939, you wouldn't have had too many fellows lining up at the old University Avenue Armories in Toronto or the Seaforth Armories in Vancouver saying king and country. They'd've been saying, "It seems like a better deal than what we've been going through in the depression." Chance to at least do something different, not be on the dole, at least feel you was parta something. But when you take that six million, and you figure 600,000 volunteered, and got in uniform, and went on their way, there was another ten percent that's maybe more impressive than any percentage anyone could apply to the whole deal and that's the 60,000 that never come back. No they never come back, and every year since then there's a ceremony on Armistice Day, November 11, at eleven o'clock – that's because of the Compiègne forest in France there, on November 11, 1918, they finally signed a piece of paper saying it was all over.

We got an awful lotta people though, men and women, who stop and remember what was going on. The whole kinda panorama, World War I, seems to be harder to shake for the fellows who was in it than World War II. At least that's the way I see it as a resulta beating my gums at many a legion hall. In the early 20s, early 30s, if you was in London, – London, England, I'm talking about – wouldn't matter where you was, the traffic would come to a halt at eleven o'clock on November 11 and everyone would stand silent all over the city.

I suppose you could say the British has got real discipline. They'll line up for three hours to buy a pork chop – not so sure we got that kinda discipline, don't even know if it's a good thing or not. But, if it's discipline, or whatever it is, respect, who knows, how do you know what it is, if it's conditioning, if it's bullshit, maybe it *is* bullshit. Maybe it was something they felt they hadda do at that time and at that place, just stand there for a couple of minutes and observe the two minutes silence.

All across Canada, from the one coast to the other, fellows would form up whatever way they could, each outfit trying to outdo the other, then away they'd go trying to do their best, usually old blazers with crests, and gray flannels, god help them if they had brown shoes or sneakers on. Last, but by no means least, the old beret or tam with the crest on it. Geez, some of the fellows have a real awkward time trying to square them old shoulders. Some guys, geez their shoulders was just nothing but human coathangers, but whatever the situation was they'd do their best. They'd strike out and try and look like what Rembrandt was trying to get at, I guess, when he painted the soldier. For just a moment they'd try and really be something. Not belonging to anybody or nothing, but being out there belonging to themselves, partners in something bigger than anybody could ever think of. Shooting their old arms and legs backwards and forwards as best they could, marching up to the cenotaph.

There's hardly a town in this country that don't have some pile of stones, or a monument, or whatever you wanna call it to the fallen. An awful lotta them got that slogan that don't seem to mean nothing no more, "Lest We Forget." Sure as hell, we forgot. We forgot on September 1, 1939 when the German army crossed the Polish Corridor heading for Danzig. We forgot then cause there was no way we could put the skids to *that* outfit. We forgot. World War I wasn't "Save the World for Democracy;" a lotta socialists will tell you it was organized and orchestrated and trouble-shot through for one purpose and one purpose along: To forestall socialism. Well, I don't know if I can go along with that, but, by geez, a hell of a lotta people tore the guts outa one another when the order was given. Millions. Millions and millions.

Many's the time I've been in Toronto for the old 19th Battalion dinner. Used to think at first I'd never make it. Often use to write, "By geez, it'll be a miracle if I can make it." Not that I was bunged up or anything, although the lower pins don't work too good, I just didn't think I'd have the strength to keep seeing the old ranks, such as they was, thin out a little more each year. Few fellows at a time. Kinda like Agatha Christie's old novel there, *And Then There Was None*, which I think was later made into a movie called *Ten Little Indians*. Sooner or later it gets down to there's nobody left. It has to be that way with any buncha fellows that decide to get together.

If you was to go around and poll everyone, they'd tell you, "O, geez, there's no way I wanna turn up at that, god I *can't* turn up at that." It's a funny thing, you know.

Anyways. I'm getting ahead of myself there. Kinda going on a tangent there. Just a bit.

Always loved music, you know, music of any kind but specially band music, military band music. The powers of one's emotions can get really tested. It's wicked in this old life, specially if someone jumps on your heart. What about the old sweats doing their best to make their old outfit look like something standing there, and many of them not too straight but as straight as they can be. By geez, the cold, wet . . . cold and wet like you get when you're standing in any old town or city that's close to the Great Lakes of Canada. I'll tell you, that's when it's really cold, that's the kinda cold not like the cold on the prairies. That kinda cold's got the damp in it that just rushes inta your bones. The lord Jesus give us pretty good minds but, by geez, them bodies he give us wasn't too good at all. They keep packing it in as the years go by, we keep breaking down, keep closing for repairs as one year comes along after another. The old mind's still going but the whole thing's hooked up to an old ticker that has to keep pumping away. Kinda gives you a fright if you study it real good. It's best not to. I think we'd like to put that way down in what the kids call the echoes of our mind. I don't think we want that kinda too much to the fore cause it just shows we're not gonna be around until hell freezes over. There's no way we're gonna make that occasion. Probably a good thing, too. I don't think I'd wanna be in on that. Can you imagine all that fire and all that coal! By the blue geez, what a sandwich to be the ham in, eh?

But I can see the old sweats, their flags all damp and mouldy, most of them swiped off the walls of churches and cathedrals across the country. Blazers and berets kinda shiny but pressed up fresh for the occasion. A lotta fellows standing there, the best you can say about them is, "Boys, I'll tell you one thing. After looking at you on parade, there's no way you can flex flab, you'd better forget it." Then, by geez, the band comes on with "O Valiant Hearts," and then they follow that one up with "Abide With Me," and you sung along with them many's the time, and now the mind wanders and the scene changes, you come together and you go away, but each time round it's one of them old services from the past. Standing there in the rain, sometimes you was lucky and there was an Indian summer, just like a late day in August. No one ever knew why; it was just as if the lord Jesus said, "Well, we better give the old bastards a break this time round." Most of the time it was colder'n a well-digger's arse in Alaska. Course, you couldn't wear a raincoat or some cellophane costume, no one wanted to look like a dildo wrapped up in Saran wrap.

Maybe some fellow's smile gets you. A quick smile after a darn good joke. There's not too many fellows can tell a joke and really kinda stick it in, and execute it, and then do a bit of a quadrille, and then a snap-to and have everyone sorta . . . you know what I mean? A good joke, if it's really laid out right, kinda gives you the same kinda snap a damn good belt does. You stand back from it and it's a moment, a moment of theatre.

That's one kinda smile. Then, there's the sad smile. You never forget a sad smile cause you seen it when you didn't want to. Someone kidded some fellow about his girl back home, and then he didn't realize the fellow he was kidding knew that that girl back home wasn't his girl no more. But, by geez, he smiles in such a way that told you that was it and, geez, did you ever wish you'd zipped up your old trap on that occasion. You didn't start saying, "Listen here, I don't wanna hear none of that." No, you never done that. You smiled but the smile was sad.

So many faces, each one of them blinking on and off, so plain and clear to see. So many moments the old mind . . . it's funny, the mind prints up pictures time and time again, but always there's the band there, and it kinda lends what you might call a frame for the whole thing, sorta beginning and an end. There they are, grinding away at "O Valiant Hearts," "Abide with Me," and then, by geez, there's the bugle, the goddamned bugle.

I'll tell you this: If you've ever put one of them cold brass pieces to your lips and tried to blow a bugle, holy doodle, just try to do it on the cold November day that ends up being Remembrance Day.

If it ain't rain, it's snow or something else, or it's on its way and, for sure, there's one thing, the wind. Boys O boys, sometimes down through the years it's been so dang cold I'd say to myself, "Fred, you gotta be losing your senses, cause here you are, old enough to know better, you gotta hole in the old right shoe there."

It's always the right one, I don't know why it is but every goddamned time there's a hole, it's in the right one. Must be sloppy-gaited like an old pacer, like old Bret Hanover, if ever there was a sloppy-gaited pacer in harness racing it was Bret Hanover. But, by geez, I'd tell myself as the water was coming through and I could feel the old foot getting damp and wet, and I'd say, "He was a champion."

Didn't matter. No matter how many times I'd bullshit myself I never quite conned myself into thinking I was a champion. I always ended up saying, "Here I am, haven't got a nickle to rub together, nor a pot to piss in nor a window to throw it out, but anyway, if that's what makes champions that's what we are." No undershirt on underneath, just a little thin setta crotch huggers, or setta shorts, an old setta flannels. By geez, there'd be a white shirt that never seemed to be in style, and then a blazer. The wind just cutting right through you. One thing I could always say: At least the hair's all in line, got her under the old beret. Some men's faces blood red – not with the booze they'd put away down through the years, there'd be a lotta guys who'd be monuments to the liquor and beer boys of Canada – but because of the raw wind. Jaws set like they'd never move again.

Then it'd come. There's no time like it in the world, and there's no better way to play it than with the bugle. No one ever says, "Ladies and gentlemen, please, ladies and gentlemen, we is now gonna have the 'Last Post'." There's never an announcement like that. If you put the whole goddamned thing into the hands of the yahoos and jackasses that run TV and radio, they'd do it, they'd have someone nip in there and say, "Ladies and gentlemen, it is now time for the 'Last Post'." No sir; that'd ruin it if you ever heard that announcement. It just happens. She starts coming out and war scenes wrapped in rain and fog shimmer, fade away and advancing with each note, come the crosses at Vimy.

You ever seen the crosses at Vimy? Ever seen a picture of the crosses at Vimy Ridge? There shouldn't be a Canadian who ain't laid his lamps on the crosses there at Vimy. There shouldn't be one soul in this country, who ain't aware of the glory that was Canada's at the battle of Vimy Ridge.

It's learning to think – that's what the whole process is supposed to be. It don't matter what wonderful university you toss up, or how many high schools with wonderful smoking rooms, bars, gymnasiums, administrators' and teachers' lounges from here to kingdom come, that ain't what education is. It's not bricks and mortar. Education is people with the brains and the minds to go at the job of opening up other people's minds. That's what it's supposed to be about.

By geez, I wish every one of them could get across to our people what it means to see the crosses at Vimy. Or for that matter, to know what the gunfire was at Ortona in World War II. Ortona. How many Canadians can tell you what Ortona means? Once again, I'll tell you they know what Nixon means, they know what Kojak means, they know what General Motors means. But do they know Ortona? I often ask that.

I remember when the prince of Wales who later became the duke of Windsor, met our boys the day they unveiled the Vimy Ridge memorial. Boys O boys, was I hot, was I *ever* hot. I'd gone to the races and took a real shellacking. So bad that the next Friday night, when I seen some of the fellas, I hadda tell them that old Freddy Dobbs would not be there in France – couldn't make the trip. Blown the bankroll, do you get the idea? Didn't have a grubstake to make it. That was one trip I really wanted to make. All across Canada, they was signing men up to make a return trip to Vimy.

The whole idea was to have a darn good turnout so that people would remember who won the day at Vimy Ridge. By the lord, you can ask the ghost of Lord Northcliffe. He pulled all the stops out when Canada won the day at Vimy. That was the biggest story in World War I in Great Britain. Yeah, when the Canadians done what the old civilizations could not do . . . yeah, *we* done it. Is it any wonder we don't know anything about it? How could we know about it when you take a look at the people who've got their fingers on the media nowadays. Do *they* give a goddamn about it? No they do not.

I can hear you saying, "Well, Fred, that was in wartime and that was a big event but how can it have any importance for the young people today?" I say bullshit to that argument. If you don't know when the hell you've got a great moment of theatre, if you don't know the hell when you're really making it, if you don't know the damn difference between a ring-round-the-rosie and getting right down to bedrock, you're not in touch, you've never touched or loved or a goddamn thing. All I'm saying is that Vimy was the payoff for Canada and, by geez, the British was big enough to give it to us. Do you think anyone's told that story in Canada? *No!* If Canadians wanna do a TV documentary they wanna pull the old death-wish bullshit out and do a big *tour de force* on Dieppe or something. That's what they wanna do. They wanna for the fifty-ninth time to tell us how we fell on our arse at Dieppe. That's Canadian, isn't it?

Geez, these people make me sick . . . we've got them all over the country. As soon as you start laying it on the line, by geez, do they ever get upset, they say, "Who's this sonofabitch putting the blocks to me?" That's a Canadian thing – as soon as someone's on to you, geez, get down behind your desk and figure out how to fix the s.o.b. as soon as you can. Cause he might be able to run rings round you, cut the ground from under you, and cut off that one thing that you're married to, that one thing that's everything in your goddamn life, that stinking, rotten pension, that goddamn little bribe, that stinking, little, miserable payoff that you can have for the resta your miserable years when you find out that the money from the insurance company ain't worth the powder to blow it to hell, that some jackass bullshitted you about years ago in the kitchen there, on the table, and your old lady was sitting there in a rocker, nodding and saying, "Yeah, it sounds like security Sam, sounds like security." But it ain't freedom.

I got one thing for all them people who never had a vibration in their knickers from one day to the next, who'd put a knife in your back just as soon as they say Jack Robinson, I got one little message for them: "Listen, you sonofabitch, you're dead a *long* time."

I was talking back there bout a big announcement interrupting the proceedings around a cenotaph somewheres in Canada. "Ladies and gentlemen, please, ladies and gentlemen." You know, when that happens it means you gotta kinda underline it and point it out to people that there's a special moment, or a special occasion coming, and what you're really saying is people's behavior ain't what it should be. Never seems to work that way with that old bugle call. For some reason, everyone, don't matter who they is, they're not programmed, they're not announced to in any way, or nothing like that, they're just sorta treated with respect, they know what's coming.

In World War I the Canadians always got the dirty stuff to do, you know. When I say "Canadians," I'm talking about two people. I'm talking about people who was second-third-fourth generation Canadians, and I'm talking about a lotta fellows came over here from Britain, right off the boat, and soon as the whole thing happened, they joined up with the Canadians who was here and that was it. There was two kindsa Canadians. You gotta give the limeys one thing; they sure knew how to give us credit. You bet your sweet arse they did.

Old Winston Churchill said it best. He says, "the Germans is either at your feet or at your throat." The Germans, in World War II after they took France – actually, when you think of it, France was handed to them on a platter, the German fifth column, and all the Vichy government supporters, and I guess the French army – there they was in the old Maginot Line and de Gaulle himself had shown the Germans, and everyone else who wanted to read his paper on the subject, how to get around the Maginot Line. The Germans followed his advice, they come right through Belgium. The French army never had the will to stand and fight in World War II.

You know, in the first war, the French finally had to say that if they was attacked by the Germans they'd stand and fight. But they told the British at one point in World War I, "There's no goddamn way we're gonna charge and start things moving any more."

Now they said that for a very good reason. When you look at a battle, the people that launches the attack is always the people that has the highest casualties. Did you know that? The defenders never have as big a toll taken on them as the people that start the damned ruckus in the first place. That's what happened in the first war; the French took such an awful pasting that they said, "Look, if we're attacked, we'll stand, we're not gonna run; but there's just no way we're gonna start any more attacks to take a few more yards of ground." That's what World War I was all about – taking a few yards of ground.

At Verdun, where the Germans introduced the machine gun, the French lost 60,000 men *in one hour*. They realized there ain't much point in trying to take them German positions and they told the British that. As a matter of fact, there was a mutiny in the French army. You know how the French dealt with that? They put the instigators in a forest and turned the French artillery on them. You can read about that in a book called *In Flanders Fields* by a guy name of Leon Wolff. That got the English so hot that the British legion banned the book in England. But it's the god's honest truth, that's what they done.

The Germans, when all's said and done, in World War II, mounted their own troops, their own guards, to guard the Vimy memorial. Course this was in line with all the Hitler bullshit about Wagner, Valhalla, and the thousand-year Reich, and all that crap. This was the kinda thing Hitler admired. So they had their own boys guarding the Vimy Ridge memorial, right throughout the entire time of World War II. They didn't want no one to touch it and no one *did* touch it.

There's 60,000 Canadian boys who never did hear "O Valiant Hearts" after it was all over. Or "Abide With Me," or anything else. And for them, that's what the old "Last Post" means. As them notes go out on the CBC TV from Ottawa each year when they capture the feeling of the event with a live telecast . . . by the way, that's usually the only real good TV you ever get is when they're looking at something right on the spot. Don't matter what you wanna look at – the Kefauver crime hearings, Watergate, or the Kennedy assassination and funeral – TV's at its best, got its greatest strength, when it's capturing the feeling of a great event. I suppose the only daily application of that, or weekend application of that, is when we have sports and they show you what's happening right at the time. The rest always has a sorta made-up connotation to it that just don't ring true.

Have you ever tried blowing a bugle on a cold November day with not a soul saying a word, no one talking, no one moving, just standing there straight as a ramrod, sometimes only a few, or, maybe, if it's a big deal, sometimes there's a thousand. All depends on where you're living. Depends, too, on what's happening. You take 1970. Right after the October Crisis, as they now call the old FLQ deal and all of that, right slick and clean across the country on Remembrance Day they had the biggest turnout they'd had in many's a year. So big that even Pierre Elliott Trudeau decided to turn out. Did you know that? He used to get the veterans hot when he'd pass that one by, but in 1970 he was there. Marched right up to the cenotaph with a Silver Cross mother and the head boys of the armed forces of Canada, put the wreath right there. Trudeau himself . . . yeah, he figured he better be there. Didn't want to be marked absent.

It's a funny thing that when war breaks out everyone runs into the churches and they often say when someone gets it, one of the last things they ever say is "mother." Yeah, I've heard a lotta fellows say that.

Heard a fellow one night in a legion hall beating his gums about being on some patrol, and, took them right by surprise, eight Germans come round the bend with their hands up. Didn't know what to do about it. This fellow who was telling the story says, "I figured we was gonna escort the sonsofbitches down the road."

All of a sudden the officer in charge of the detail says, "Give it to them!" The fellow telling me the story says he looked up at the officer and says, "I beg your pardon, sir, what are you saying there?" The officer says, "I said give it to them!" Fellow standing there with a Sten gun. He obeys the order, puts his finger on the trigger, and all them eight Germans go down in about a second or two. Odd one lunges forward . . . not to attack, just a kinda death spasm.

Guy telling me the story says he hears one of the Germans

moaning like, trying hard to talk through the blood that's gushing outa his mouth. Fellow kneels down, puts his ear near the German's mouth. The dying German is trying to say, "*mutter, mutter*" – German for mother. ●

11
The
Phantom
Pisser

First of all, I wanna point out that one of the roughest things about staying in the old Ford Hotel, the old Bay Street riding academy, was dealing with the house rules where pets was concerned. I had Robarts with me, you know, and by geez, I had to sneak him out on a daily basis, cause everyday you gotta water your dog. It's not an easy business in a hotel that's got a buncha elevators and a big groupa lobby generals, glued to their chairs, taking a look up every time that elevator would stop. Just like spearing fish in a barrel, their lamps would be right on whoever was coming and going. There wasn't too much them birds would miss, I'll tell you that. But I used to fix up a buncha shopping bags, get some old Dominion and Loblaws shopping bags, and stick old Robarts in, with his keester and hindfeet in and his forefeet out the top.

But the bags made in Canada . . . I get awful discouraged with us at times. We can't even turn out a shopping bag that can withstand the calla nature of a good twelve-pound dog sitting inside it. By geez, I'd be coming down in the elevator, and old Robarts would get short taken, or he'd turn one loose. He might've had a few fresh fried eggs for his breakfast. Loves eggs, and he's a smart dog. Knows enough to know that a fried egg's got to sit right up in the pan. Kinda eggs you get outa barnyard where the chickens is walking around in their own shit. Not these vicious businessman eggs we got nowadays. Poor bastards oughta be liberated by the SPCA, and we could send all the eggs they lay to the armed forces, and use them for ammunition in World War III for all the taste they got.

But geez, Robarts would get into the eggs, he'd get a real spell on, and you couldn't satisfy him, and you'd be cooking the eggs, and after a while, boys O boys, the air would be blue. O, it would be wicked. He'd just be sitting in a corner driving them, and you'd say, "Listen, you've just got to go out and air yourself."

So, we'd take him down the elevator. Everyone would know; they'd miss some fellow who'd be stepping out, say smuggling some friend in for a little bitta companionship, O, they'd miss that. And there I'd be, caught right at the door with the old bag in a desperate state, and Robarts with his front paws sticking out, and looking up at me. Geez, it would be wicked altogether.

We used to have a lotta laughs down at the old place though. One thing about the Ford. You could march up and register, and get a room for $2.50, and you could stand there, and sign the register with a monkey on your arm, and there wouldn't be any smart alec yapping about, "Now, is it Mr. and Mrs . . ." and all this and that, and all that drivel they used to put you through before the motel come along. Actually, before Holiday Inn and all the US chains got up inta Canada . . . funny thing, Canadian business can barely even run a hotel chain. You take all the hotels that have burst on the scene across the country. Once you wipe the railways out, and a few other outfits, they're pretty well US chains. It shows we can't even do that. It's just fantastic when you think about it. But I get an awful kick out of that.

And then, of course, the old Ford hadda be tore down, a real historic site, when you come to think of it. What a great location. Used to be just a few blocks walk from the old University Armories . . . geez, they tore that down after a great fight to try and preserve it, which was lost by all hands. Imagine that, the old armories. They've got the stone from her over at the Moss Park Armories. It looks like a potato warehouse or something.

They took the stone from University Avenue to Moss Park and laid it in there to try and commemorate a little bitta history. But when you think of all the boys that's marched through the doors of the old University Avenue Armories in Toronto, by the blue geez, all the fellows in the depression who went through that door in 1939 when they thought the next best thing to do was to join up. It was a lot different, of course, in 1939-45; it wasn't so much for king and country, it was to save your arse because there just wasn't nothing doing. Chinatown was between the armories and the Ford, and you had any number of places where you could get real good grub for far less than a dollar.

But I finally struck out for the east enda Toronto, down around what was the old Woodbine, now it's called the Greenwood Racetrack, and finally found a room in a house there. Seemed like a nice sorta landlady. I remember a fellow come, to rent a room, and said his name was Oliphant. By geez, it was a funny deal that went on. He hadda spell it out, and she kept calling him Elephant. And he says his name's Oliphant, and spelled it out, and by geez, she says to him, "All right then, sounds to me like it's all right."

Then he said, "Well, you asked me my name, now I'm going to ask you what's your name?" She said, "Siddi Bathom". Well, he thought, that must be s-i-d-d-e-e, then Bathom. Well that's sort of a hyphenated deal, like an English name, you know what I mean. Bathom. That could be anything. Could be B-u-t-t-u-m. By geez, she's really got a name that's spelled S-i-d-e-b-o-t-t-o-m. Sidebottom. Ain't that wicked? There they are, one's elephant and the other's sidebottom, and it's All-I-Fant, and Siddy Bothom.

Anyways, her sister is a wonderful woman. I still don't know her first name. We've always called her Mrs. Bovary, and of course, when she kinda overreaches herself, you know, she gets to be pretty bossy. Sometimes she butts inta things, and that's when we hang

"Madame Ovary" on her. She puts up with old Robarts' barking, and you can use the phone in the front hall, and one thing and another.

Geez, I'm minding the time, one night there, I had a setta pants hanging up over the door, and Winnie was tossing and turning and couldn't sleep. Kinda bad night for the sinuses. There's an awful lotta people who breathe the wrong way; they breathe through their mouth insteada their nose, they gotta have an operation or something I don't understand. But their sinuses get all riled up, especially with the industry pollution, which, of course, is the holy air that business gives us. It's the wonderful air we breathe, for the reason that business is functioning to employ people. Did you know that?

In Canada, part of the golden age of B.S. is to let people know that business is in business for the purpose of handing out jobs. They don't even have the balls to stand up nowadays and say that they want to have a profit for a darn good product, or a darn good service they're rendering. Cause most of them don't have a good product, and most of them don't know nothing about service. As a matter of fact, they get their shorts in a knot the minute you get your lamps on them and tell them they don't know nothing.

I get a great kick out of saying in the United States there'd be some concern for the customer, and then you see these little middle-class minions, you know, and they're the real fellows that are being gypped by the gyp-your-neighbor system, and they've swallowed holus bolus the golden age of B.S. And they're the ones who'll defend it to their death. They're the funny ones. They're about half a rung up from the absolute rock, stony, bonkers bottom, but they're acting like they gotta share in it. And they're getting fleeced morning, noon, and night, and they get hotter'n a firecracker when you tell them to open up another wicket.

I get more kick outa going inta bank around lunch time. I know half the girls is out having their lunch, and saying, "Are you gonna open any other wickets here?" Air Canada's run an operation for a decade with a slogan, "Next wicket, please." You know, they couldn't give a damn how long you stand around, cooling your heels, because they've had the computer boys in, and they've shown them. The computer guys do everything. The machine figures out you can keep the suckers waiting any length of time.

Go to the supermarket and put your lamps right on them. Just stand at the express counter, and just have a look at how they keep people waiting. That's all part of the great golden age of B.S. Make the suckers wait. They'll stand there, carrying their bags of crap, and then when they step up, they pay. They wait on themselves, and then they wait with the order in their mitts. It's terrific. I love the way it goes.

But, by geez, what was I getting on to? I don't know how I got onto that string, but, geez, I . . . I remember now what I was talking about . . . I'd had a real bad day at the track. And like most horseplayers, I wasn't up to a third-degree examination, you know what I mean? And when I come along I figured well, we'll just tell her that we, you know, b.a.e., broke about even. Well, geez, I guess it didn't have too good a ring to it. Anyways, Winnie was tossing and turning in her bunk and just couldn't take her eyes offa them pants hanging over the door.

By jeez, she gets up and the next thing I hear is, "Fred, do you know you've gotta dollar thirty-five in your drawers and you had a whole fistful of money at noon today? What happened?" The best defence in the world is to get hotter 'n a firecracker. Well, I started shooting my mouth off, telling her to mind her own business. Old Madam Ovary, she laced her army boots on right up to her armpits, and she come running down, wanting to know what the fuss was about. Twenty minutes later we're all sitting around the kitchen table laughing, making a pot of tea, and kinda got it all ironed out. Winnie's a pretty good old skate.

It's kinda nice being in a rooming house, you know. O, there's lottsa bad rooming house deals, too. I've been in a lotta places where, geez, they had a line painted on the bathtub, they had rules for the place. We used to always write all sortsa obscene things on the lista rules down in the main hall there.

I think the first rooming house I was ever in was when I come back from France in 1919 after the war. I come back just about the time the North West Mounted Police boys, the army police, come home. They brought them home, and shipped them right slick and

clean out to Winnipeg cause of the strike was on, and the army
fellows wasn't about to get outa the service, and then have to face
the civilian boys. The army boys wasn't cutting the mustard to suit
the government around the time of that strike. As a matter of fact,
that's what saved the mounted police's arse. All of a sudden
someone in Ottawa realized we'd better have a federal police force.
"Geez," somebody in charge says, "this volunteer army – we had
the boys down at Shilo just about ready to stand them all down. As
soon as we call on them for an emergency – we had the same
situation as was happening over there in Russia."

The soldiers soon get the message that these was their own kind
there and they wasn't about to obey their officers. Geez, that
reminds me of an awful funny fellow in the rooming house I was in
in Winnipeg. I think it was on Langside, not too far from Portage
Avenue. I hadda little room there. Geez, we had more orders of the
day there: no pets, no visitors after 9 PM. Can you imagine anyone
running an outfit nowadays, trying to get away with, "No visitors
after nine o'clock"? O, geez, of course we broke *that* rule. The
springs on the beds would always tell an awful story. Geez, it'd
sound like . . . holy doodle, we won't go into that.

There was this fellow. He was a real funny guy, not a bad fellow
at all. He was . . . you got the idea he was kinda stuck on himself,
but he wasn't really. He was an officer in the army out there, and
he'd gone to private school. One night we were all sitting around
talking. He told the funniest story that god ever told the other
fellow about. He was telling us that at the school he was at, they
was real real strict, and you hadda stay in your room with your
door shut, and then a bell would ring, and it was time to open your
door up, and stand outside your room. Then everyone trooped
downstairs. And they filed in for grub, and, of course, someone said
the grace. And it was almost like a logging camp, and there was no
talking during the meal, nothing like that.

Well, anyways, on this day, there was a big commotion around
the washroom. Kids being kids, of course, it don't matter whether
they're born with a silver spoon in their mouth or not, they're still
always giggling and laughing if there's a big washroom event. I
think it's the Anglo-Saxons . . . we all sorta go back to our toilet

training. Everyone was saying, "Step right up and have a look at this."

He says his curiosity got the best of him, so he run down the hall, and went inta the washroom, and, by geez, there in one of the toilets was a sight that he never thought he'd ever lay his eyes on in his life. It was almost like a Ripley "Believe it or Not." There was a footstool in the toilet there that wasn't going to go down unless you got a fireax and bust it up.

After all the laughing, and snickering, and shuffling around, and everybody playing carnival barker, "Step right up and have a look at this," and so on and so forth, the assembly bell rung, as he tells it, and about seventy of them all lined up outside this old schoolmaster's living room-office deal he had there. They waited for him, and finally he come out, and finally they stopped their giggling, and he quizzed them pretty close. And his interrogation was plain and simple. He wanted to know who'd put the stool in the toilet. Well, by geez, he went from one boy to the next, seizing each one by the lapels, shaking them up real good and demanding to know, "Did you put the stool in the toilet?"

Nobody owned up, of course, so finally he said, "Well, I'll give you all ten minutes up in your rooms, and I don't want anybody to open their door except the guilty party, and whoever that is, he's to come down to my office, and the rest of you stay inside your rooms until further notice." Geez, the time runs out and the bell rings and they all reassemble again. This time he's absolutely wild, comes right over the desk, seizes each kid by the lapels: "Did you put the stool in the toilet?" "No sir."

When I heard it I started to laugh. I says to the officer, "Did he have red hair?" He says, "Yes, he had red hair." I said, "I think I know that guy. He used to shout at me years ago. He used to shout at me and say, 'You're British and don't you ever forget it!'"

Anyways, the fattest kid in the school, god love his heart, he owned up to it and confessed. Of course, that brought the house down. Then there was a pause, you could hear a pin drop. The old schoolmaster, suddenly all of a sudden there's a heart of gold beating in his breast. He says, "You're not well, son. You're not well, you're sick. You're a sick boy. Yes, we've got a sick boy here.

You're going to need to go to the infirmary." Always remember that story.

We hadda funny lotta people in that rooming house, and so many times we used to sit around, so many of us from different parts of the country, and talk.

Sooner or later, someone from Nova Scotia would bring up the story of old Angus McAskill. Well, he wasn't too swift, Angus McAskill, and everyone knew it in Liverpool, or Halifax, or wherever it was, on the docks because he was always down there. What he was best known for was being one hell of a giant of a man with the strength of several horses.

One day a fishboat come in, and some of the boys in the boat began to tease him. There's a great big anchor right at McAskill's feet there. The guys from the boat say, "I'll bet you couldn't put that anchor up on your shoulder and hold it there." Angus says, "What's the bet fellows? Put the anchor up or whatever it is?" One of them keeps clearing it up, and he says, "I'll bet you couldn't hold that anchor on your shoulder there." Anyways, a few of them got together and it took all their strength, and might and main, to lift that anchor up on McAskill's shoulder. Then they just stood back and laughed at him, because they knew he wouldn't be able to get that anchor off.

Angus finally hadda get it off, it was getting awful heavy. If you was standing around with a thing like that on your shoulders, you'd know what I mean, one of them iron anchors. Geez, when he tried to take it off he tore his collar bone, it hooked him, like, and he died right there on the spot.

True story, god's honest truth. And you know, when I heard that story I couldn't help think of the cruelty, the kinda thing where you wonder why is man so cruel to his fellow man. Here's a fellow, never harmed nobody. But they hadda have their joke. They hadda prove they was a little better'n him. Maybe that's what it's all about. But I never forgot that story. I always used to think, "Wouldn't it have been wonderful if someone could've come along, strong and big enough to take that anchor off his shoulders, and catch them birds who done that, and teach them a lesson or two?"

I think one of the sad things for an awful lotta people who's on in years is that somehow, some way, they've never really learned to be on their own. Loneliness is a sick thing. Course, the TV saves an awful lotta people nowadays. There's an awful lotta people kinda married to their TV. That's their company. They switch that on and, by geez, if they don't have Lloyd Robertson at eleven o'clock when they go to bed, there's something wrong. Imagine that. Kinda speaks volumes, don't it?

I think it's gotta do with this dang business of as soon as we're on this earth, we're running around seeking approval from the people that has brought us into the world. That's awful important to get their approval. And then we start out making friends, and we go to school, and seeking approval is important there. Then there's the whole business of religion and church and so on and so on. This whole dang thing of, "Love me, and like me, and I wanna kinda have part of you, and I wanna sorta own you a little." We've got a lotta things mixed up in that, you know, and I think you see it when you're in a rooming house, where there's gotta be a little give or take, where everyone's gotta kinda . . . you know, you can't help yourself to all the sugar one day, you can't take all the hot water. You gotta think of the other fellow.

On the other hand, you've got your own bunk, and you gotta live a little by the rules when you got one of them places. I remember old Morris, who was a bookmaker's telephone man in Vancouver, I told you about him before. He used to say to me, "Geez, Fred, hadda wife and three kids in Winnipeg, and in the depression when everyone had the arse outa their pants, I was making good money as a cattle buyer, down in Chicago, making real money, just living the life of Riley, hundreds of dollars." And then, he said, he blew it all on the horses, and ended up in Vancouver. He said the best decision he ever made was to find an old hotel that hadda bitta heart.

The old Austin in Vancouver, at Davie and Granville, it hadda bitta heart. That's in downtown Vancouver. We used to have a lotta laughs there. There was an old Chinaman and his wife used to clean up the beer parlor, and every so often you'd hear them take to shouting at one another, and then you'd hear a couple of blows. He'd come out, and Morris'd say, "What's the matter Jack?" (His name was Jack Wong.) And Jack'd say, "No good woman, beat with broom, beat with broom. No good woman."

I remember one night Jack come running into the lobby about three in the morning. He says, "Come quick, come quick." So we run inta this great big beer parlor. Geez, it must've been about a 400-seater or something. It was a huge place. He took us right inta the women's washroom there, and there was one poor old soul, she was still holding it down on the throne. She hadn't budged. Scared the hell outa Jack. He wanted to know what to do. Geez, I sent for the old fire department.

I remember one time I was working down in the front office. Morris phoned me from his room and he says, "Fred, there's some fellow, and he's running round the halls here without a stitch on, and he's using all the ashtray stands set by the elevator as a urinal." I says, "Oh for god's sake, that's ridiculous." Anyways, I run upstairs, and, by geez, I'd run back down to the lobby and the phone'd ring and Morris'd say, "He's on four."

So I'd get on the freight elevator, and go on up to five, then steal down the stairs to four. Geez, I couldn't catch him. But boys, there was a bitta evidence there, right in the sand, one of them cigarette things you plunge your cigarette inta the sand. This is about an hour and a half this is going on, and we're raising a hell of a commotion. All of a sudden, a window opens up right in the well rooms, the inside rooms, and a voice calls out, "Ain't you sonsofbitches caught the phantom pisser yet? Because if you ain't caught him by now you're never going to. There's no way he could keep going."

I remember another time I was in the lobby there, not a soul around. About four in the morning. All of a sudden, the door opened from the elevator, and out got a couple, not a stitch on either one of them, just drunker than hoot owls, laughing their heads off. And they both said, "We come down to join you."

The old boss of the Austin was a sharp old fellow. To cheer him up in the morning I'd say, "Well, we're half full. Pretty good night." He'd say, "What do you mean half full? We're half empty."

One night I'm there on the desk, minding my own business.

There was four hotels on the four corners of the block. This was the soft underbelly, you know what I mean, of Vancouver. An awful lot like the old Ford in a way . . . all them places, a bit dingy, sordid. You wouldn't say anything was really first cabin. The phone rang and it was a fellow from across the street. He says, "Fred, it's Wilf from across the street, from the Blackstone." Actually it was called the Martinique in them days. Geez, *any*thing went there. Boy, you'd get up to certain floors there, I'll tell you . . . O, holy doodle, what a place that was.

They was just catering to the fishermen, the loggers, and the miners, who hadn't been around the women for a year and a half to two or three years, and they'd come into town, and, O geez, they'd be feeling pretty good. A lotta them they wiped out in phony crap games, and the next few days they'd be sitting around, stony broke, muttering about the rotten goddamn DPs who're the only people who've cornered all the money, or they'd be blaming the Jews or somebody. What a laugh that used to be. I used to say, "Oh, come on, give over, don't give us that kinda horseshit." We'd start toe to toe with some of them fellows. O yeah. Imagine a fellow working a year and a half to two years, and then he falls on his arse in a crap game where the dice is loaded against him. He's that big a jackass to get inta a thing like that, and then he's sitting around muttering about some poor fellow who's over here from Roumania who's at least saving his money, and trying to buy a rooming house or a little business, working his arse off, and here's a guy hating his guts. Actually, he's hating himself, you see, but he's gotta hate somebody else. That's back in the days when they used to call someone from Europe a DP, a displaced person.

You know, you'd think all them people from Europe wanted to come over here. Well, they come over here cause they had nothing there. Now most of them did not think the streets was paved with gold, and here's our own fellows, our own people just hotter'n a firecracker at them. Used to make me wonder.

I was talking to a fellow in Vancouver not too long ago, and he's telling me, he says, "You know, Fred, it's an awful thing, I hate to say it, I hate to admit it. You know me, I've been in the army with you, we've been through a lot of rough, tough times in the hotel business now. But give me a buncha Indonesians, or Koreans, or Vietnamese, or Japanese, or whatever. Geez, they're polite, they're honest, they're hard-working sunsofbitches, and they don't steal from the customers.

Give me a buncha Canadians, they've got a lotta goddamn lip, half of them are just passing through, they're going on to a bigger job somewhere else. They don't bust their arse, and a hell of a lotta them will swipe every towel, mat, bar of soap, and bottle you got in the place unless you nail it down."

It's sure an indictment against these stinking, provincial, education systems we got, cause I'll tell you one thing that's come outa them, and another thing that's come outa the great wonderful Christian religions we got in this country, and I'd have to say the families to some extent, too. There's no real philosophy when you get right down to it – it's gyp-your-neighbor, Buster. It's screw your neighbor as best you can, and move on to the next objective.

Anyways, this fellow from the hotel across the street phones me up and he says, "Fred?" I guess he figured I was dozing. Half the time on the night shift you could take a bit of a snooze as long as you had the door set up. We had a real big, heavy, squeaky door, and as soon as anyone would come in, geez, it would wake up the dead down in the basement. Quite often some of the cops would stop in and have a drink down in the basement. They could hear the door open. In fact, they knew when their sergeant was coming through that door, cause you could tell his hob-nailed boots, and the way they'd fly out that door. Of course, they'd hightail it down the back way through the basement, and out inta the alley, and and then come through the front door innocent as all get out, and say, "Hi Sarge, what are you doing?" He'd look at them and say, "Listen here you sonsofbitches, my name's Tucker, not Sucker. You get the hell back to that car." O geez, he'd be hot.

I'm getting off. I'm going round Cape Horn again.

This fellow rings up one night, he says, "Fred, there's a couple of fellows with a great big box. Geez, the size of it. It's the size of about four iceboxes all welded together. Real heavy and they're heading your way." He says, "Don't let them in. I told them, I says we was all full up." That's an old dodge, you know. I looked outa the window, geez, I seen this great, big paira Hoosiers. Geez what a paira rough stones they was, dragging this huge, great, big box and they go right inta the hotel across the street. I think it was the Cecil . . . not sure: the old mind ain't so good as she used to be.

I seen the fellow, god I started to laugh, although I was scared, the old ticker was starting to beat. I knew I was next. I was the last one on the list, that wasn't too hard to figure out. I could see him shaking his head from right to left, from right to left, and there was a bitta hesitation. Finally they come outside and pick the dang thing up and start heading straight across the road. By geez, I thought, "What the hell harm is there in letting them in?"

Well, they come in and, boys O boys, they're ten sheets to the wind, the paira them. One of them says, "Wanna room for two weeks." And I says, "All right, fellows." Then the guy announces to his buddy, he says, "Well at least we found a white man." I got the key out and I said, "Well, let's get upstairs. Have you got any baggage?" Geez, if looks could kill I'd have dropped right there in my tracks. The baggage, of course, was this quadruple icebox deal they had. That was it.

One fellow's pants was fastened on with a piece of rope. The other guy, the spokesman like, he says, "How much is it gonna be?" In them days you could getta room for about nine dollars a week, and so I says, "Well, I tell you what. You'd better give me eighteen dollars and a dollar for the key." He dives inta his pocket there, and he's got a great big roll would choke a racehorse, and takes a couple of elastics off it, hands me a twenty, says, "Keep the change." I says thanks and okay. And upstairs we go.

Never seen hide nor hair of them for the two weeks. Never seen hide nor hair. Now I know they had a couple of lady friends up to their room because Kale, the bellhop, told me and one of them phoned down to say he couldn't find his teeth. Kale went up, and the four of them was all mixed up in what looked like at least twenty-five meals that had gone inta the room over the week, all lying in the same bed, the sheets was gray as a British Columbia sky, and here was the teeth sticking in his arse. He'd lost them and sat on them, and they was right there, and Kale says, "Here, you're sitting on them, they're right there." They all started to laugh, and

Kale says, "God, you need a clothes peg on your nose to go inta the place."

They kept ordering jars of pigs' feet. About four in the morning you'd have a cab driver from Diamond Cab run in the door . . . Yellow Cab it was, I guess . . . "Where you going?" "Oh, I gotta take these four jars of pigs' feet upstairs."

Come the day for them to check out, they come downstairs, all dressed to the nines, new suits on. The two of them looked like Little Lord Fauntleroy. Butter wouldn't melt in their mouth. Laid down a hundred-dollar bill on the counter, and said, "This is for the bellhop." Another hundred, "This is for the people on the desk. We've enjoyed being here and we'd like to reserve a room when we come back to town in two years." And out the door they went and down the street and no one ever saw them again.

We went upstairs and looked into the icebox deal they had, and, by geez, they had about a hundred bottles of wine. The worst kind of varnish remover god ever told the . . . In fact, splitting the shoulders of a bottle of Derby compared to the stuff they was drinking would be like living high off the hog. Anyways, that's what they had.

I remember another time we played an awful joke on a couple that, they'd had a honeymoon . . . imagine having a honeymoon there. Anyways, they had a honeymoon and no one seen them for about five days. Didn't hear a noise, not a peep. They had the "Do Not Disturb" sign on the door, you see. Geez, the old gal on the desk, she were a wonderful old woman, she sent up a pint of blood. They hit the ceiling and the four walls . . . were they ever hot over that.

It'd be terrific fun listening to the lobby generals. Old Morris'd sit there with some of the logging camp hiring bosses. There used to be one who was dressed in what he called Dack flannels, and Morris used to get an awful laugh outa that. And geez, did he ever get the guy's goat one year when the queen was coming. That's when the *Vancouver Sun* wrote a big story about the "carnival atmosphere" that was gripping the city. "The city waited with an air of anxiety and anticipation for the arrival of her majesty the queen mother," or whatever it was. Geez, you could've took a poll anywhere, I tell you, anywhere in the beer parlor in that joint, and said, "Are you anxious? Has a carnival atmosphere come into your life?" and you would've got a resounding, "Absolutely not." This is the kinda stuff that just rots my socks.

But Morris one night was teasing this old fellow, this old hiring boss from the Powell River company. And he really got at him real good, too. Morris says, "Well, when the queen comes by, she'll be able to look up at hotels here at this intersection and see all the butterboxes hanging outa windows. Someone can explain to her 'That's refrigeration, your majesty.' Then she can look at all the kids the schools have assembled along the sidewalk to cheer her. School's out."

This guy was a real royalist. He got up, and he says, "God damn you, get up to your room or I'll place you under arrest." Can you imagine that? Morris started laughing and he went upstairs, and for weeks after he'd phone down to the desk, you'd be busy as hell, and this voice would say, "Get up to your room or I'll place you under arrest." Click.

All that stuff kept us busy. I always noticed when a fellow retired, a lotta fellows from the railway used to retire and take rooms there. That's when they was all in but the boot tops. That's when it was game over. The old horseplayers, they all lived on. They were all sitting there arguing about this or that, one year after the next. They was always there. But the old guys who had nothing to do but sit in the chair, and stare out the window, and probably most of their lives it wouldn't have mattered who'd worked with them. They'd be talking about how rotten the job was, and how glad they'd be when they could get away from the whole dang thing to retire, and so on. Looking forward to something that killed them and never even knew it.

How many people like that have you seen in your time and you wanna say to them, "Listen, Buster, you'd better shape up because you're betting on something that's going to do you in. You think it's going to be a bed of roses and it ain't." We don't realize that unless we have these things to do every day, tough as they might seem, or dreary or whatever it is, or boring, they're the things that keep us going. They're the things that without them the boredom riots would break out. I'm always glad, you know, that I've always wanted to be around people. I guess you could say that my university has been conversation with people. That's where I've picked things up. Been able to sit down and beat my gums with people anywhere, any kinda people. That to me is a form of university and I wouldn't trade it with anything in the world. ●

12
A Great Day for the Calgary Chamber of Commerce

You know, if you asked a hundred different people how they got hooked on racing, you'd get a hundred different answers. And I've always liked to ask the next person how they got the old habit of flirting with the angels, as we used to call it. But for me it was real easy.

I used to laugh at my old man and my mother because they'd quite often go into Hamilton on the old Grimsby-Hamilton radial car, on the old street railway to the races at the Hamilton Jockey Club. And I used to always say to them, "Geez, what are you going there, and spending your money, and losing your money for?" A trip to Fort Erie for them was a real big deal. I can remember, as a little boy, always trying to go along with them over to Fort Erie. That was a real junket to go there. They'd go on the train, of course; I think it started out from Toronto and it would stop along the way and they'd be down at the old Beamsville station. They've just taken her down there now, you know.

My old man got real mad at me one day, he says, "Fred, you're always shooting your mouth off about how going to the races is wicked. We don't know who's put this stuff inta your head, but you've got too much to say about your mother and about me going to the racetrack. There's no harm in it." Then, he give me a long lecture about how the king of England loved being at the races, and didn't ever want to be anywhere else, and all that sorta thing. So he says, "Go and find out about it . . ."

I took his advice, and one day I was getting up real early in the morning to go to Hamilton to see the horses training. It was August, and gosh, it was hotter'n a firecracker. No, July it was, around Dominion Day. And he says, "Fred, where are you going?" I says, "I'm going to Hamilton, some of the fellows are going over to watch the horses, we're going to stay over there for the day." He says, "I told you to find out about it, not to *live* there." And I guess I never looked back from that time forward.

When I count up all the schools I went to and all the racetracks I went to, I have to conclude I'm a racetrack inspector. I'd have to say I am. And I'll tell you it's been a wonderful show wherever the hell I been. One thing about racing, unlike all the other sports in the world, you don't have to see the very best, you don't have to see the very best ball teams, you don't have to have the big league, you know what I mean. You don't have to have the real pros.

You can go to Red Deer, Alberta, and see a buncha Indian boys riding a half mile bareback. Seen it myself. Wherever you are, and there's horses coming over from the barns to saddle up, and parade round, and then go over for the start, and get on running . . . by geez, I don't care, it's just a feeling. it's a whole routine that just seems to work no matter where it is. That's something that the guys who put on the racing game don't seem to know. They're a funny lot anyways.

The great thing about racing is, it's survived all the people who's tried to screw it up. Funny thing about racing. I mind the time I was in Calgary, and I think his name was Cross, James Cross, I'm not sure of that. He had the Calgary Exhibition Stampede

Company, that put on the Stampede at the old Victoria Park racetrack grounds. They now call it Stampede Park, the old Victoria Park track's gone.

Geez, they decided one year to charge the Indians admission money to come inta the grounds. And the Indians used to be at least half the thing. They was the people that give it a real flavor and a real feeling. You'd be coming in from Banff, Alberta, heading towards Calgary, and if it was just coming up Stampede time you'd see the whole Stoney Indian tribe on the highway, strung out bout a mile long. Big occasion for them. On their way inta the Stampede grounds, setting up their village.

You'd come up from Sweet Grass, around that way, down near the border there, and geez, you'd see the Sarcees and the Blood Reserve . . . you'd see all them Indians on their way. It was a big event and a wonderful thing to see. And they'd cook right out, and dance, and talk to everybody. You don't find them Indians running around saying, "Don't be half safe." They loved it. It was a chance for them to bring their world next door to our world, and there was no attempt, for once, on the part of us to tell them what they should be doing. There was none of this awful guilt feeling the white man has for what he'd done to the Indian. None of that.

You'd see faces a century old. You knew damn well when you looked right up at someone that he was a fellow who maybe straddled a horse pretty near a hundred years ago. And seeing the poor Texas whiskey dealers coming over the border, you know, to Fort Whoop-up or something. That's a great story.

I think by the time the North West Mounted Police got to Fort Whoop-up, or whatever the hell it was called, a force of 600 I think, struck out from the Red River Valley, 300 deserted on the way . . . note *that*, you won't find it in your Canadian history books . . . when they got there there was one old Texas Hoosier, and three Indian women sitting in the fort. That was it. The others had all gone. This was supposed to be the big battle that was going to preserve the west for queen and country. What a joke that was.

Anyways, I'm getting ahead of myself. They decided to charge the Indians to come inta the Stampede. I think it was 1948, around there. Around the time old Jim Fair won the King's Plate in

Toronto with Last Mark. I was out that way around Stampede time. By geez, the word bout the admission charge spread fast from one band to the next. They decided the night before the Stampede in downtown Calgary, right outside the Palliser Hotel, and railway station there, right in the old downtown area, they decided to stage a rain dance. By geez, they held their rain dance, and do you know, it rained every damn day of the Stampede that year, and you can look it up in the record books. They blew a fortune. O, I thought that was wonderful. I love that.

I can still see them all dancing there . . . they had the most fascinating way, they'd anchor one foot on the ground, and take the other and do bout 1,2,3,4,5,6 quick steps, then anchor that foot, then 1,2,3, . . . and they're all going, "Heeeeey hoooo." Geez, that was terrific. They put the kibosh on that. That's one time the Indians let the air outa the white man's rubbers.

I can remember the fellows with the racehorses running at the track. Geez that track . . . O boys, was it ever muddy and it was just real, thick, gumbo muck. And horses like Double Dot and Air Cadet and Last Sun . . . I can just close my eyes and see the day old Emile Roy rode six outa seven winners on the card at Borden Park in Edmonton. Got nipped by a nose in one race. By geez, that was quite a feat.

The Canadian jockey, George Woolf, was known as the Ice Man. And you know Smokey Saunders come outa Calgary and Johnny Longden, he was born in England. Not too many people know that, but he come to Alberta, worked in the coal mines when he first was in Alberta. He was awful small, Johnny Longden, you know, never took a back seat to anyone. I mind the time I was hanging over the walking-ring rail at Santa Anita, for my money the greatest racetrack on the North American continent – just outside of Los Angeles in a little city called Arcadia. Geez, Johnny Longden, he and Willie Shoemaker had both finished up the racetrack, or down the racetrack, on a pair of horses trained by Willy Molter, the great Willy Molter, who also rode out in western Canada.

There's another fellow, Willy Molter, one of the great public-stable trainers in United States horseracing. Geez, Shoemaker and Longden was on a pair of horses he'd saddled in what turned out to be a prep race for a big rich stake coming up the next weekend. Only a five-horse field, and here they are, two of the top jocks in the world, coming home fourth and fifth. And geez, they was real hot favorites to do something. The people was all riled up, they was hotter'n firecrackers, some of them. You know, some people get right crazy by that kinda stuff. They can't just stand back, and grin like they've seen it from one year to the next.

I mind the time I'm there, looking over the rail at the horses in the walking ring, and the paddock judge says, "Riders up," and all the riders do a turn round, and start heading out through the crowd on their way out, and onto the track, and geez, this woman . . . she was hotter'n a firecracker . . . she'd been running around telling everyone what a disgrace it was, and it was time the attorney general come down from Sacramento and close the whole goddamn place down, and she was going to be writing to her congressman, and so on, and so forth. She shouts at Longden, "You couldn't ride a toilet seat, Longden." Old Johnny Longden, the Pumper they used to call him, Moneybags Longden, he takes a look at her, and everyone looks at her, and looks at him to see what was going to happen, and all of a sudden he looks at her, and smiles and says, "Maybe not, honey, but I sure could ride you." I think they fined him five hundred bucks for that, "for conduct not in the best interests of racing."

That puts me in mind of old Ray MacNess, what a great fellow he was, and a wonderful announcer for the CBC Pacific region. He was a dedicated horseplayer and he told the story of one time, in the dirty thirties, he and his brother was racing outa Hastings Park they used to call it, the old half-miler. It's now Exhibition Park and it's not half mile no more.

They went broke early in the card, so they put their heads together, and decided to go out up to Commercial Drive, up near the old York Theatre there, their mother's place, and get her old washing machine outa the basement, and get it downtown, and get it into what was called the San Francisco Tailors, which was a funny name for a hockshop, but it was one of the big hockshops in Vancouver.

They get home to their mother's, and she's out. They go down

inta the basement, and they disconnect the old washing machine.
The way Ray told it, he says, "You can imagine how heavy one of
them old army tanks must be cause I'll tell you this washing
machine, it was five of them." By the time they get to the car stop
to get the old Commercial Drive BC Electric streetcar, they was all
in but the boottops. Anyways, they lifted it on board. Everyone's
staring at them, thinking they was stark raving mad. They finally
get downtown, get off the streetcar, roll it across the street into the
San Francisco Tailors, and the guy says, "How much do you want
for it?" Well, of course, it was the depression times, but even then
it was worth a lotta money and Ray says, "I spoke right up and I
says ten dollars." Pawnbroker says, "I'll give you three and that's
it." Three wasn't going to do much good at the racetrack. They
went back to the track, and the horse they bet on bust his leg right
in fronta the stands.

That wasn't the end of the story. Ray was at work the next day,
and the phone rings, and it's his mother, and she says, "Ray are you
busy?" Well, he was kinda busy, he was just about to go on the air
and do the news. So he says, "I'll call you right back." He knew the
heat was on, he knew what was coming, so as soon as he done the
news he called her up. She says, "Ray, they tell me the both of you
was in here, and you went out the door with my washing
machine." So I guess the neighbors had spotted them, and Ray says,
"O gee, Mom don't worry about it. It wasn't working too good, a
short or something. We figured we'd get it downtown and get it
fixed for you."

As time went by she kept ringing up, where the hell's the
washing machine. Then it got to the point of, "I've gotta do the
washing. I can't do my washing." Well, he finally got the dough
together, and they bailed the washing machine out. They rolled it
on the street, they went about seven blocks with it, rolled it into a
garage. And they got some guy there, and got into cahoots with
him, and he welded a little metal box on the bottom of it, right
where the power plant deal was. That cost a few bucks. And then
they rolled her out to the streetcar.

He said the whole day went down the drain by the time they got
back out. They showed it to her, she was right out on the porch,

with her arms on her hips looking just like a mean sergeant major. So, he said, "Mom, we got this deal put on, it'll make things go better, you won't have the trouble with the power cutting off." That was all well and good, and they had some coffee, and cookies, and pie, and so on, and she fed them up real good. They lived down in town, you see, they'd left home by then.

Ray's back at work the next day, the phone rings just as he's going on the air to do the news, and the fellow says, "Ray, it's your mom, and she says it's real important." Ray says, "Well, tell her I'll call her back." Guy says, "No, she says if you wanna do the news tomorrow, you'd better speak to her now."

Ray gets on the phone, he says, "Hello mom." She says, "Don't 'Hello mom' me. What was that jackass box you welded on the bottom? It fell off." Well, the gig was up, and as Ray says, "By gosh, I sure had to sit down and confess all. And it's a funny thing, when you start telling one lie, you got to tell another, and then another." He says that taught him a lot. He figured he'd had all the devotion anyone was ever going to have for buying oats and hay, and that putta stop to the whole thing. No more of that bullshit.

I was talking to Boomer the other day and he says, "Fred, they're saying on the TV, and it's in the paper, what a tough row this is to hoe for all the MPs, this capital punishment thing and how to vote. It's put an awful lotta them in a terrific bind. They've gotta free vote this time round, they don't have to vote the way their bosses want them to, they can vote the way their own conscience dictates. But on the other hand, they know back home this is a real hot-fire emotional issue, what with all the mail they've got, and all the stuff that's been in the papers from one week to the next. Usually there's some police chief somewhere calling for a return to the noose, the strap, and the paddle. It's pretty tough to kinda sit down and keep cool."

I says, "Boomer, for god's sakes, if they're upset . . . good. I'm glad. It's about time I read that our elected representatives was upset. I've never seen it in print before. Show it to me, I'll pin it up on the wall. I hope the suckers absolutely sizzle in the pan. I hope they're going home, everyone of them, tonight, right at this very moment, saying, 'O my gosh, I'm just torn apart over this issue.' I hope the old space between their ears is really given a jolt. That's the best news I've ever heard. I didn't know anything ever upset any of them. I never knew. I think if anything has come out of this whole schmozzle on this subject, that's the best news I've ever heard.

"And while we're on it, never mind whether we should abolish it or keep it, never mind going into all that, and going over that old tune again. If we're gonna abolish it, if that's what's gonna happen, then let's do what they do in Japan. Let's just make owning a gun against the law, and that's the end of it. And let's not have no more ammunition sold over the counter to anyone unless it's someone in the armed forces or the police."

I mind the time a fellow was telling me round Prince George, on one of the lakes there, they set down and examined the marks of pontoons from a couple of big float planes that had come right in. They went inta the woods and there was a whole stack of caribou with their heads cut off. Piled up. Thousands of flies and thing creeping all over them. Somebody just come in and hacked the heads off as trophies, loaded them on to the planes.

Do you know what was worse? All sortsa bullets just lacing them up and down, back and forth. Hunting animals like that, with automatic guns from planes. If anyone's going to hunt in Canada they should be told, "You gotta go down and buy a bow and arrow, fellow." If I could train bears to handle a bow and arrow, I'd love to shoot most of the hunters right in the arse. Now, that to me is where the animal has some kinda chance, and where the hunter is showing some kinda skill too, and he's got to steal through the woods the way an Indian would. Course, half the Indians in the country wouldn't know how to hunt now. They're the first to admit it. Now that to me is hunting. Not some big, trussed-up goddamn, corseted business jackass up here from over the border, all fulla booze, with an automatic gun, going in low over a lake, and spotting one of them creatures standing by the shore, and landing and lopping his head off.

Just as you come in the front door of my rooming house, that's where old Madame Ovary has her headquarters. That's so there's no way you can tiptoe across the threshold there without her light switching on, and a big flood of light coming out on your shoes. She's in on everything. But that's all right, she's worked hard, it's her own place. She gets pretty tough on the rent, too, you know.

Course, Boomer, who has a room at Madame Ovary's, too, was in the Ford with me. He hadda room at the Ford, and we used to pull the wool over E. Y. Crack's face. O, many's the time. He was the old credit manager down there. He'd ride you pretty hard. Used to put plugs in the doors if you got behind in the rent. They'd come up and jam one of them little plug things right inta the lock so you wouldn't work the lock, so you'd have to go downstairs. Then there was no way you could kinda tiptoe through the lobby like Sylvester the cat. You hadda get down there and say, "How come you plugged the door of my room?" O, many's the time I've seen guys as guilty as sin, all fulla bullshit, sitting there talking about how in the morning they was gonna go see the manager. There's nothing funnier than a fellow without a leg to stand on, bluffing and trying to intimidate someone.

Course, behind the counter there's some fellow who's been over here from England for the last fifty years, but he's still acting like he just got off the boat, telling him to lower his voice. That was always good for a few laughs, but Boomer was always pretty good at fooling old E.Y. Crack. He always used to buy him a few beers, get him sorta loaded, he'd ask him to come up to the room. After the Ford closed down, we seen old Crack down at the track a couple of times.

It's a funny thing, you know. When I think back over the years, there's some people who've been awful lucky, talking with me about horses. It's something you can't explain, but whenever you run inta them, maybe you've talked about the horses, or a horse in a certain race, don't know what it is, but you've steered them right.

Then there's god knows how many more people, O, dozens and dozens, don't matter when you see them, there's just no way you'll ever come up with a winner with them. But they'll still keep asking. And boys, did we used to lay some of the . . . Boomer played a rotten trick on old E. Y.

One day he says to me, "Fred, I'm awful sick of old E.Y. Crack, you know, he's plugged the door about three times in the last two months. He's leaving notes, and threatening to take the stuff outa the room, and so on, and so forth. He's here, so you'd better say hello to him." And he's there, and then boys, his head's up, and he's on his way over to the table. He sits down. This time Boomer lays a horse on him. Well, I looked at the *Form* and I just had to laugh to myself. Here was some sucker that couldn't have outrun a fatman. It was a five-year-old maiden and in racing that's a sexy name for a horse that . . . either sex . . . it ain't never won a race. In fact, around the racetrack for centuries now, they've said, "He'll never break his maiden," meaning he'll never win.

Boomer gives him this thing, and we don't think no more on it, boom, down it comes, pays $112. Well, Boomer didn't have a nickel on it, I didn't have a nickel on it. Crack comes over and he figures we both cleaned up. There's no way he's gonna believe our story that we didn't have a nickel on it. As a matter of fact, we didn't want to say we didn't have a nickel on it. We let on we had it. We wanted to make out we knew what was going on.

Geez, that got us into more trouble. The chain of events that sprung from that incident. First of all, he thought Boomer was a genius. And he just couldn't understand why we couldn't keep the rent up on a regular basis. But we'd given him that, so the pressure was off for a little while. But it didn't last too long.

Boomer's always had this old death trap of a car, you know, he's had a Terraplane and I think it's a 1933, what a model it is. Nowadays it doesn't matter what you're buying, it's getting tougher all the time to fix anything on your own. It don't matter wheather you're buying something for hi-fi, or your car, or whatever it is. You gotta take it in, and they gotta put their own mitts on it, because the manufacturer's the only person can pry the damn thing open, and the only person who's got the slippery parts that fit it. But Boomer somehow can just go to any old junkyard and just keep the thing running. But we've had a few bad spells with her. I remember one time we missed the double at Fort Erie; we broke down outside, I think it was Fruitland. I've often thought them people had a lotta courage to name a town Fruitland, especially in this day and age.

Maybe our cars don't run too good but they ain't alone. It's a sad thing in Canada, despite the fact that we've got all the easy access for travelling . . . I'm not talking bout the trains. I think the railways has hadda kinda diabolical plot for years against the railway passenger. Probably the thin edge of the wedge for the railways getting outa the passenger business was when they started forgetting to put paper in the washrooms. That was the first active intimidation.

And just you wait until Air Canada gets its leprous hands on some of them old railroading ideas. By geez, if they ever pull the paper in the sky there'll be more'n shit hitting the fan. Of course, if god meant us to fly he'd never have given us Air Canada.

By the blue geez, I'd better rest this tired old mind of mine or Winnie'll raise holy old cain. I can just hear her now, "Come on, Fred, give over now. Get yourself home here and behave yourself."

Course, I'm an awful lucky fellow. I still got my health . . . you can't buy good health, you know, she's still not for sale. A lotta rich millionaires ain't around to tell you that one.

Winnie's looked after me real good. "Come on, Fred, you gotta spell on now. You get yourself home here and stop all this mollyhoxing around. You gotta rest that old frame of yours or it'll be game over."

She's right, you know, gotta rest the old frame. Time we pulled up and headed for the old stall. Time to get on home, maybe home to Beamsville. It's quiet there, the air's cleaner, nothing like clean air. In them big cities . . . Vancouver, Montreal, Toronto . . . they're all starting to breathe in the stench of their own garbage. Wicked altogether. But that's what's happening. Politicians still don't have the guts to tell the industry boys, "Enough is enough." No sir, it's still open season on people's bank accounts and their lungs and livers. The old gyp-your-neighbor system keeps on bobulating along.

But Winnie's right, we should all get some rest, don't cost nothing, and it sure helps keep the old "Closed for Repairs" sign away from the door.

Better give old Madame Ovary a ring at the boarding house to tell her I'm going home to Beamsville. Maybe not. She'll wonder what I'm gonna do there, she's still after me, you know. I'll have to give old Keith Rich a call, too. Let him know everything's gonna be all right. Let him know I'm not down at the old boarding house, I'll be down in Beamsville. Geez, I might try to breed old Duddie's Adios just the once more. Might get her to take this time. If it don't pan out this time it won't be the enda the world and it won't be the start of one either.

You know something? We're all gonna be dead one hell of a long time and, it's funny but there's one word that still scares the hell outa us, a four-letter word. No, not the one you might think there, it's L-O-V-E. You know, they say the hardest line for an actor on stage to say is, "I love you."

Now, I'm gonna put on the old heel swifters and fleshpads and get my old arse home to Beamsville.

We'll be talking to you. ●